Higher Education and
Public International Service

Higher Education and Public International Service

Papers, Addresses, and Discussion Summary of a Seminar Sponsored by the Commission on International Education of the American Council on Education in Collaboration with the Department of State, March 1967

EDITED BY ELIZABETH N. SHIVER

AMERICAN COUNCIL ON EDUCATION • WASHINGTON, D.C.

Foreword

Recent changes in the meaning of the word *seminar* are demonstrated by the fact that an important meeting held in Washington last spring under the auspices of the Council's Commission on International Education and the Department of State was called a seminar. No graduate students were present, and no professor was in charge of the discussions. Instead, it was an assemblage of very knowledgeable persons concerned with the topic, "Higher Education and Public International Service." The meeting was arranged to further discussions between two sectors of society that are recognized as having a growing interdependence.

The subject, the future of international intellectual communication, was one of real consequence to both parties. It entailed prepared papers, addresses, and lengthy discussions.

Many of the participants expressed the hope that the American Council on Education would bring the deliberations of the Seminar to the attention of a much larger group of interested persons through publication. The present volume is a response to that desire. We trust that it will contribute both to a sense of urgency in rethinking the future of international educational and cultural affairs and to a greater understanding of the dimensions of the task.

Logan Wilson, President
American Council on Education

August 1967

Preface

Anniversaries can be celebrated in various ways. The most common, perhaps, is by memorializing past achievement. An alternative option is to seize the occasion to look to the future. This volume of papers reflects a seminar conceived for the latter purpose.

The Seminar was planned and conducted by the Commission on International Education of the American Council on Education, with the collaboration of the Department of State. It was held at the Department March 24, 1967, approximately twenty years after the inception of the Fulbright Program, and was attended by approximately one hundred persons of broad experience in international education. The participants included both public officers and members of the academic community. The discussions were greatly stimulated by the active participation of the Secretary of State, the Assistant Secretary of State for Educational and Cultural Affairs, and the Assistant Secretary for Education of the Department of Health, Education, and Welfare.

The particular concern of the Seminar was the next decades of international intellectual communication, an aspect of international polity so manifestly furthered by the Fulbright Program. The discussion was grounded on the extraordinary growth during the past twenty years of the United States' commitment in international educational and cultural affairs.

Although the dialogue was not meant to concentrate upon the record of those two decades, the highlights of that record formed its foundation. They deserve brief notice at the outset of the proceedings.

Since the end of World War II the Fulbright Program, and companion programs of federally sponsored intercultural relations, have made it possible for literally thousands of scholars and students to move back and forth between this country and other nations. Substantial numbers of American academic institutions, and their men, were enabled to enlist in human resource development and institution-building all around the world. The great adventure of the Peace Corps was born, and matured. Although other efforts developed within both the public and private sectors, it can be fairly said that these three major thrusts were sufficient to signify a serious and permanent new dimension to public policy.

As the period 1946–66 drew to a close, both the Congress and the Executive evidenced a desire to look ahead. Most notably, the Congress authorized substantial new federal investment to strengthen our academic resources in international affairs, and the President advanced a many-faceted program for new government commitments to international intellectual communication in a special message to the Congress, February 2, 1966.

The International Education Act of 1966, perhaps the most far-reaching of the new governmental initiatives was, among other things, evidence that twenty years of increasing intercultural commitment had demonstrated how great was the need to expand the literacy of the American people in international affairs. Solidly grounded in experience, the clear intent of the Act was to marshall United States resources to meet this need in a systematic way. It was enthusiastically endorsed by the nation's colleges and universities.

The context of the Seminar, of course, was influenced in major degree by the vast changes which had taken place in the world since the close of World War II. All other considerations aside, these changes make it imperative to rethink the objectives and the means of conducting international educational and cultural programs.

The pattern of change is perceptively treated in the background papers and discussions of the Seminar. The main threads of that pattern are worth brief notice at the outset, however.

The post-World War II generation witnessed the passing of historic empires, in a political transition the more remarkable for its relative containment of revolution. As a consequence, in part, definitive changes took place in the effective power balances of the world; and the United States and the Soviet Union emerged as the new centers of overriding political power. Just beyond the clear horizon, by 1966–67, lay the possibility that the new balance might be further altered by a resurgent Communist China.

A new blend of economics and politics was, meanwhile, made visible in a surge toward numerous new and independent nationalisms. Taking place predominantly in the two-thirds of the world most economically impoverished and politically immature, this movement more than doubled the initial roster of the United Nations. The sheer weight of numbers in the General Assembly created an increasingly evident handicap to constructive action.

Throughout the period, the commanding role of science became discernible on every side; but the implications of scientific progress were threatening as well as salutary. For the first time man was enabled to reach beyond his world into space. Yet, for the first time also he fashioned and took uncertain command of the weapons of his own destruction.

Advances in medicine and public health greatly reduced human mortality. Yet, this fact, coupled with rising birth rates, began to press catastrophically against the world's food supply, threatening mass starvation in many areas. Pressure mounted to limit the population and increase the production of food. The first pressure cut across religious and cultural inhibitions of long standing in many countries; the second was itself inhibited by massive movements of men away from the land and into the cities, all over the world.

And, as the corpus of knowledge geometrically increased, it became ever more clear that no comparable progress was being made in perfecting man's instruments of control over his expanding knowledge or, for that matter, over his political behavior.

Both within and between cultures a new virulency of race-consciousness arose, presently etching in strident protest, and even in blood, the fact that two-thirds of the world is predominantly nonwhite and, by the standards of the advanced minority, dispossessed politically, economically, and culturally.

By 1966–67, these massive and fluid forces compelled the taking of new sights across a wide spectrum of national aspirations, not least in the area of international relationships. This Seminar was conceived as a measure of stock-taking in international educational and cultural relations, as a means of adjusting its sights to the realities which had emerged in a generation, and which profoundly affect its future.

It is not greatly difficult to assemble a group of thoughtful and concerned men for such a seminar. This was done. The greater challenge lay in the need to provide a setting in which they, as members of organized social mechanisms, could be persuaded to rethink fundamental premises. The federal government and the academic community, with which most Seminar participants identified, are in many ways the conservative custodians of past reality. Neither is easily persuaded to modify its premises or its ways. In this sense, the Seminar was bound to swim against a tide of habit, alike in conceptualizing new goals and in devising new means for their attainment.

To establish a base for forward consideration, and to provide as favorable as possible a climate for constructive discussion, three background papers were commissioned for the Seminar, and distributed in advance to the participants.

Consideration of the shape of the future demands in intellectual communication as viewed from the academic vantage-point, was accepted by Dr. de Kiewiet as his assignment. Professors Adams and Jaffe agreed to address the same problem from the point of view of government, Professor Adams' membership in the United States Advisory Commission in International Educational and Cultural Affairs constituting an unusually favorable milieu within which to formulate such a prognosis. Professor Harbison was asked to consider the need, and the bases, for new strategies with respect especially to educational assistance to developing countries. The gist of the discussions generated by these papers forms the body of these summary proceedings. (Since it is hoped that this volume can be useful in generating further discussion, an additional paper is included which was authored subsequent to the meeting by the Seminar Chairman, Dean Stephen Bailey.)

The Council is heavily indebted to many persons for helping to make this Seminar possible. Particular mention can only be made of a few. Wise preparatory counsel was provided by Department of State officers, members of the Inter-Agency Council on International Educational and Cultural Affairs, the United States Advisory Commission on International Educational and Cultural Affairs, and the Board of Foreign Scholarships, among others. Very special appreciation is acknowledged for the active participation in the discussions of Secretary of State Dean Rusk, Assistant Secretary of State Charles Frankel and Assistant Secretary Paul Miller of the Department of Health, Education, and Welfare.

It would have been literally impossible, however, to have managed the close working collaboration on the Seminar between the Department and the Council without the invaluable assistance of Messrs. Frank Hopkins, Francis Colligan, and Mrs. Elinor Reams, of the Department's Bureau of Educational and Cultural Affairs. They extended to this joint effort the ready and helpful assistance upon which the ACE has come to depend in its day-to-day relationships with the Department.

Richard A. Humphrey, Director
Commission on International Education
American Council on Education

August 1967

Contributors

WALTER ADAMS
Professor of Economics, Michigan State University

STEPHEN K. BAILEY
Dean, Maxwell Graduate School of Citizenship and Public Affairs, Syracuse University

JACOB CANTER
Deputy Assistant Secretary of State for Educational and Cultural Affairs, U.S. Department of State

ROYDEN C. DANGERFIELD
Associate Provost and Director of International Programs, University of Illinois

C. W. DE KIEWIET
Chairman of the Overseas Liaison Committee and Consultant to the President, American Council on Education

CHARLES FRANKEL
Assistant Secretary of State for Educational and Cultural Affairs, U.S. Department of State

PAUL R. HANNA
Director, Stanford International Development Education Center, Stanford University

FREDERICK HARBISON
Director, Industrial Relations Section, Princeton University

ADRIAN JAFFE
Professor of English and Comparative Literature, Michigan State University

PAUL A. MILLER
Assistant Secretary for Education, Department of Health, Education, and Welfare

DEAN RUSK
Secretary, U.S. Department of State

Contents

The Modern University

A number of years ago, Albert Einstein attended an International Conference of Academicians in Geneva, Switzerland. He opened his address with a note that the Conference was meeting 700 years too late. He pointed out that an academic conference held in the thirteenth century would have been conducted in a common language, Latin, and would have been based upon common assumptions about the universe, the earth, and about man himself. In the twentieth century, he concluded, there is no common language of scholarship, and mankind's assumptions about God, nature, man, and society have become almost endlessly divided.

Stephen K. Bailey

We are today all too consciously aware of the price of this diversity and dissonance. If the Holy Roman Empire was neither Holy, nor Roman, nor an empire, it did at least symbolize a series of attitudes, assumptions, and concepts which allowed nationalism to climb its way up the cliff of history roped, loosely at least, to certain moral and religious precepts which were widely shared. The adumbration of international law by Hugo Grotius in the seventeenth century was in fact based upon ethical postulates which Western Christendom had developed over four centuries of national evolution within an internationally accepted body of normative principles. If the immediate cause of Grotius' humane tract was the unrestrained barbarity of the Thirty Years War, his positive norms were based upon what E. H. Carr has called "a sense of obligation deriving from the unity of Christendom and the validity of natural law. . . ."

Looking around us today, we see a world far transcending the Christendom of Western Europe; we see a bevy of positive national laws in place of a single natural law; we see vast areas of the earth governed by men who reject the notion of transcendent legal principles. Without common moral and legal assumptions, the nations of men find modern instruments of international organization and technology largely incapable of resolving the violent con-

1

flicts of our age. Even simultaneous translation is ineffectual without a common sense of meaning and value.

Those who search for international order are faced with the prior necessity of rediscovering a common discourse—a way of talking meaningfully across international boundaries and cultures. A world community starts and dissolves in the minds of men. If our prime task in these sullen and critical days is to search for a new order—an order which transcends national boundaries—what are the moral and intellectual tools at our disposal? Are there modern counterparts to the medieval synthesis? Are there notions, ideas, ideals which can serve today as the basis for an international community? And are there institutions and instruments capable of disseminating, propagating, and refining such notions, ideas, and ideals?

The answer to these questions, I believe, is yes. And this affirmative response is based upon my assumption that the modern university is in fact the secular church of this age, and that what is taught in the modern university constitutes the only corpus of universal knowledge and values in the entire world. This is a shorthand way of saying that the ultimate international responsibility of the modern university is world order—a world order based upon a common language of science, a common appreciation of cultural diversity, a common assumption about the necessary limits of willful sovereignty, a common belief in the dignity of the individual mind and spirit.

I am contending that mankind can no longer achieve an ordered community by arms or naked power politics. It can save itself only if universities succeed in developing an invisible and worldwide college of reason which can overcome the irrational parochialisms of a divided world. Only then can armies be transformed into benign police; only then can politics be contained by universal law.

What are the assumptions that link universities together across national and cultural boundaries?

The first assumption has an eighteenth century quality: it is the assumption of the universality of reason. This belief in reason, as Carl Becker once pointed out, became the Heavenly City of the eighteenth century philosophers—a restatement and echo of the Ciceronian and Augustinian view that natural law was in fact "right reason." It was this consummate faith in the capacity of the unfettered human mind to conquer the bastions of man's constraining traditions which led Thomas Jefferson to swear eternal hostility to all forms of tyranny over the minds of men. Free inquiry, logic, and open discussion would ultimately lead to man's triumph over nature, over traditional prejudice and superstition, and over himself. The relative tranquility of international politics in the nineteenth century following the Congress of Vienna, and under the maritime shield of Pax Britannica, led many to believe that a rational millennium was at hand. August Comte, Charles Darwin, Louis Pasteur, Thomas Huxley, John Stuart Mill, T. H. Green—these men were the symbols of evolutionary progress towards universal reason and reciprocal political obligations. The productive triumphs of the industrial revolution were the palpable results of the human mind at work. The discordant prophecies of Marx, Nietzsche, and Freud were viewed with disdain or dismissed as the rantings of warped intellects.

The cataclysmic nature of the twentieth century has all but destroyed man's faith—man's beautiful faith—in the power of reason. World wars; economic depressions; social, economic, and political revolutions; racial and religious passions and prejudice; crime; violence; dictatorships; genocides; neurotic ideologies—these have been the raw and bitter winds of cyclonic passion which have marked the days of our years. And these winds have been reenforced by the invention of technologies of destruction which make the apocalypse pale before imminent possibilities.

If the eighteenth and nineteenth centuries rediscovered and reified man's capacity for reason, the twentieth century has rediscovered and reified man's capacity for irrationality and bestiality. In many nations even the basic institutions of rationality—the universities—have been made tools of national passions and purposes.

But wonder of wonders, the possibilities of reason have survived. The quiet powers of rationality are perceptibly on the move. To paraphrase William James, these powers work from individual to individual, creeping through the crannies of the world like so many soft rootlets, or like the capillary oozing of water, yet . . . if you give them time [they] will rend the hardest monuments of men's pride.

While politicians rant and armies clash, the international laboratories and academic colloquia of the world are knitting the fabric of man's universal brotherhood. Increasingly the test of the validity of knowledge is not whether it conforms to religious or political dogma, but whether it conforms to accepted canons of scientific proof. We say nothing of importance when we speak of a *Soviet* scientist, an *American* scientist, a *Brazilian* scientist, a *Japanese* scientist. The adjective is simply not descriptive. The only important adjectives, and ones which can be conferred only by academic peers, are words like good and bad, careful and sloppy, imaginative and stodgy. There is in fact a universal language today. It is not

Latin, or English, or Russian. It is symbolic logic, seen in its most pristine form as mathematics. This is not the mathematics of projecting the number of angels one can place on the head of a pin; it is the mathematics of calculus, or probability, of inference. It is the root base of all of the technological triumphs of our age. It is the most coherent and most widely accepted language of the university in every land and in every culture. It is the gold standard of the world's intellectual currency. The first great international responsibility of the modern university is to refine and to universalize this language—for in the short future it may be the only tool available to enable mankind to continue the construction of the tower of Babel. It symbolizes, even if it does not encapsulate, the divine element in the world; for as Plato once held, "the divine element is not coercive but persuasive." One cannot coerce another to accept a mathematical syllogism; but if reason is left unfettered, one can persuade another to accept it. The university can be truest to its international responsibility when it fosters those powers and instruments of reason which can most readily transcend national and cultural differences. Physics, mathematics, chemistry, biology, astronomy, and their application through agronomy, engineering, medicine, applied oceanography, and space exploration—these know no boundaries of geography or culture. They involve a universal discourse of reason without regard, as the saying goes, to race, color, creed, or national origin. These are the subjects of the universal university, and their promise for human betterment is incalculable.

One could settle for this definition of international responsibility, if it were not for the fact that we are more sophisticated today about the human condition than were the eighteenth century rationalists or the nineteenth century optimists. It makes little sense to posit universal, invisible colleges of scientists and mathematicians moving at the speed of sound from one university laboratory or colloquium to another, if such itinerancies are threatened with interruptions of nuclear explosions or even of denied visas. Man's passions, prejudices, and parochialisms can blot out the signals of reason. They are static-producing; they can jam the frequencies of intellectual discourse. They can interrupt the application of science to problems of human amelioration. They can distort man's conquest over nature and turn the miracles of technology into instruments of wanton carnage.

So universities have a companion and even more immediate international responsibility. In addition to being repositories and developers of universally accepted knowledge, they must be catalysts of multinational and multicultural understanding where intellectual and aesthetic agreements are not secure. They must be centers of relativism as well as centers of certainty. They must moderate differences as well as affirm agreements. They must develop antennas of empathy as well as interlocking tentacles of proof.

If the modern university is universal in its science, it also tends to be parochial in its politics, aesthetics, literature, and ethics. Most products of American higher education are woefully ignorant of the history, culture, and aspirations of other peoples, especially non-Western peoples. We have lost that sense of transcendentalism that enabled Ralph Waldo Emerson and his Concord colleagues to relate unabashedly to creative humanists in all climes and times. The astounding and heartening reality to those who take the time to read about and to observe other cultures is not only the glorious diversity of mankind, but the wholeness—the holiness, the oneness—of man's essential nature; the commonality of fears and displeasures, of joys and aspirations, of passions and rationalizations. Sir Christopher Wren reflected identities with, as well as divergencies from, the anonymous architect of ancient Mesopotamia Ziggurats. An Aztec temple is not a New England church—and yet it is. A No drama is not an English miracle play —and yet it is. A Persian rug is not a Bayeaux tapestry—and yet it is. An Indian sari is not a mini skirt—and yet it is. African drums are not symphonic timpani—and yet they are. Buddha is not Christ —and yet he is.

The international responsibility of universities is to search for the thematic oneness of man while valuing the beautiful diversity of thematic expressions. For example, expressions of courtesy vary enormously across the face of the globe; the notion of courtesy is universal. Expressions of art are varied as a field of wild flowers; the notion that some things are more beautiful than others is a common value across all lands and cultures.

If we can only teach and learn that the things that divide us also unite us; that underlying all human behavior are common forces, needs, and aspirations, which emerge in different forms of expression but which link each human being to all other human beings in an integrated mutuality.

The second international responsibility of the university is, then, to probe for an understanding of the similarities which undergird mankind's wonderful diversities, and to dwell on how to preserve the latter while reenforcing the former.

When the similarities are understood, the construction of a viable world order becomes possible; when the diversities are illuminated and valued, freedom under law becomes a universal promise.

But neither a world community of science, nor a universally shared understanding of cultural similarities and differences, is adequate. Universities have an equal international responsibility in describing, analyzing, and constructing institutions, processes, and norms of civil relations—economic, political, and juridical. The humanistic preconditions of world law are not the same as the law itself. A course in the theory of international trade is not a substitute for the hard bargaining and compromises of a Kennedy round of tariff negotiations. A learned treatise on international law is not the same thing as the resolution of international conflict by the Security Council or by patient, multilateral diplomacy. The behavioral sciences and a variety of professional schools in such fields as law, public administration, industrial management, and international diplomacy must help to develop human capacities in the fields of institution building and conflict resolution. A world community does not mean the end of bickering and tension. It means, to paraphrase the great words of Lord Balfour, that the world has become so fundamentally at one that it can safely afford to bicker. It means that institutions and habits exist for accommodation and for the settlement of disputes. It means that tension-filled interfaces can be resolved with justice and without bloodshed. The social sciences, pure and applied, analytic and normative, must become truly internationalized in content and must be geared increasingly to techniques and stratagems of problem-solving. The fact is that mankind still has a difficult time in attempting to govern itself. Its institutions of peaceful conflict resolution are still rudimentary. On a vast scale of international academic cooperation, of academic exchanges, of intensive and extensive research, of international apprenticeships, of technical assistance, of language institutes, we must set about the business of qualifying this generation and coming generations for the bristling and bustling international marketplace of politics and economics which we have now collectively entered. Mechanical means of transportation and communications are on our side; what we now need are the minds, the skills, the ideas, the will to use these technological wonders as instruments of cooperation and of peaceful conflict resolution.

What, then, are the international responsibilities of the university? I have mentioned three: refining and extending the common intellectual base of science; illuminating the cultural similarities and differences of the world—valuing and sustaining both; and improving the human capacity for institution building and conflict resolution.

But if all universities do is to extend the range and utility of human knowledge and skills, they will have missed their most compelling function. The ultimate international responsibility of education is to affirm and to restore man's sense of his own nobility. The insistent message of the prophetic geniuses of history is that there is a qualitative difference between man and beast—that man has the capacity to enter into a special relationship with the universe and that this special relationship is man's glory and meaning. The Psalmist asked the appropriate question and affirmed the appropriate answer:

When I consider Thy heavens, the work of Thy fingers, the moon and the stars, which Thou hast ordained; what is man, that Thou art mindful of him? and the son of man, that Thou visitest him? For Thou hast made him a little lower than the angels, and hast crowned him with glory and honour.

We, in this century, need no blind poet to remind us of our Paradise Lost, nor a William Blake to illuminate the convolutions of hell. We in this cataclysmic epoch know how far man has fallen. But to fall is one thing; to despair is quite another. We despair, and we have forgotten why we despair. Fundamentally, we despair not because of external horrors or existential suspicions of personal mortality. We despair because we have forgotten our place in the universe, because we have become so preoccupied with man as animal and man as object that we have forgotten man as creative spirit and man as noble subject. In the name of realism we have fashioned a monstrous caricature. We have accepted Jonathan Swift's view of man as "Yahoo," while ignoring the nobility which Swift transferred satirically to the horse but which can be discovered only in the heart and mind of man.

Why do we forget so easily? What has happened to us in this generation that we ignore the capacities and promises of man? We study the ashes and ignore the phoenix. We dwell upon our failings and shrug off our triumphs. We see London through the eyes of Hogarth and pretend that Christopher Wren never lived. We have become aliens in our universal home because we have become aliens to ourselves. We are storm weary. The turbulence of violent change in this century has plunged us—like a frail aircraft —into a towering cloud of spiritual darkness from which no escape seems possible. One of the difficulties is that we have not read enough history to recognize both the transient nature of all thunderheads—no matter how massive—and the buoyancy of the wings of the human spirit for negotiating attenuated stress. In disproving progress we have forgotten the reality of the Pilgrim's Progress. Writing in the dingy jail of Bedford, John Bunyan, in his great allegory, lets Christian fall into the clutches of Giant Despair. Giant Despair's castle (which Bunyan astutely labels Doubting Castle) has a black dungeon with no possibility of escape. But finally the prisoner plucks from his own bosom a key called promise and opens wide the dungeon door into a larger life.

Every university is in part a Doubting Castle, for one of a university's prime responsibilities is to doubt. But the other great responsibility of a university is to affirm, to establish fertile hypotheses—including fertile hypotheses about the nature of man.

Surely this is our supreme contribution to our students and to each other: to rekindle excitement in life by touching the fire of man's promise to the wick of learning. Far too often we have settled for less. We dissect man. We put calipers upon his littleness. We mechanize and quantify him. We spell out with excruciating candor his palpable failures of nerve and intelligence and benevolence—individually and collectively. We thrust our telescopes into the blackness of infinity, and poke our cameras into the fitful trackings of subnuclear activity; and we ignore the wonder of what we observe and the even greater wonder of the observer's eye and mind. We measure IQ's and dismiss as irrelevant the quotients of beauty and goodness.

The ultimate business of social science, and of all education, is human freedom. If human freedom means nothing but the sad and sorry flow of existence upon a well-documented darkling plain, the charge to university graduates should be to push the button when they have the chance. If the human race has in fact been caught up in an irreversible ebb tide, if Matthew Arnold's transient mood at Dover Beach has become an eternal reality, then it is irrelevant whether the missiles fall. For the option is an endless melancholy, a sullen ennui—deaf to the song of the thrush, blind to the evening sky, and indifferent to the creative wonders of man's mind and hand.

Universities affirm today, as they always have, the promise of human life. We see citizens and public officials, not as instruments of survival or of a vegetable security, but as instruments of human freedom. The Good Society is an arrangement of institutions and laws which helps to free man from bondages of fear and loneliness and injustice and from the crushing impersonalities of life. It is a society which promotes all that is ennobling and creative in the human psyche. It is a society whose ultimate dividends are joy and variety and vitality within the bounds of community. It is a society in which government postulates man, not as he has been or even as he is, but as he can be.

The job of a university is to educate men and women to see reality as the God of Genesis saw the chaos, as clay to be worked, and above all to recognize that the working of the clay is part of the reality, and that the clay is to be worked for man's individual fulfillment.

If we pass on to our students an easy optimism unrelated to the intractabilities and complexities of modern life, we do a disservice. But if we cannot pass on to our students hope and faith— a mounting excitement about the future possibilities of man— nothing we do will be of much account. To educate young people to manage the public affairs of an ant heap is hardly a calling worthy of the name.

The great philosopher king of prewar Czechoslovakia, Thomas Masaryk, once defined our supreme task for us. Writing in the twilight of his years after decades of struggle in the harsh arena of public life, Masaryk summed up his philosophy in the following words: "You see how it is; the method must be absolutely practical, reasonable, realistic; but the aim, the whole, the conception is an eternal poem."

And what is this poem? Its essence is to be found on the walls of the foyer of Maxwell Hall at Syracuse University—words taken from the Oath of the Athenian Citizen—words which must forever be the motivating theme of universities the world over:

We will ever strive for the ideals and sacred things of the city, both alone and with many; we will increasingly seek to quicken the sense of public duty; we will revere and obey the city's laws; we will transmit this city, not only not less, but greater, better, and more beautiful than it was transmitted to us.

But in our case, read "world" for "city" throughout.

Common Concerns of
The Government and the Universities

Dean Rusk

I am delighted to welcome you to the Department of State and to express my very great interest in the common concerns of universities and the government in the international area. My interest in the university and world affairs antedates by some years my present responsibility. Most of you may have seen the report, *The University and World Affairs*, which a group of us put out in 1960. I should like to comment briefly on certain matters of considerable importance in which the universities and government are very much involved—and, indeed, most of our citizens are very much involved. I have in mind especially two or three areas where I feel we could get more help from the universities than perhaps we are now getting.

I think we have perhaps not caught up in our public thinking with the extraordinary pace of change we are now experiencing. There are many ways to illustrate it. I have now dealt with more than four hundred foreign ministers since I have been Secretary of State—eighteen from the Dominican Republic alone. I have lived through more than fifty-five coups d'etat somewhere in the world. In the beginning—during the first two or three—I was very much disturbed and excited. Now they are getting to be a little boring. Of those fifty-five, I can tell you, the CIA did not cause even one.

We are going to have rapid change ahead, and it puts a great premium on the clarification of guidelines of policy. Those guidelines are and ought to be utterly simple. I think one of the tasks of the universities ought to be to help us sort out those guidelines, analyze them, examine them, and make them known to our citizens. For example, it is a fundamental proposition that agreements ought to be observed. That is a proposition that is at least 2,000 years old. If that were not the general practice among nations, the world would fall into utter chaos.

We are parties to more than 4,500 treaties and agreements. Those agreements tend to give order to an otherwise turbulent process. They tend to make it possible to predict how nations will act in a given situation, and, in one way or another, order much of the daily lives of ordinary men and women.

The simple notion that governments derive their just powers from the consent of the governed not only is the most revolutionary idea still abroad in the world, but is a major guideline of policy to those who are making decisions in government. It explains why we have welcomed more than sixty new nations into the community of nations since 1945, why we are deeply concerned by what goes on behind the respective curtains, why we are dismayed by our own shortcomings here in this country in living up to the great commitments of our Constitution, why we are so much more intimate with other democracies than we are with dictatorships, although there are some dictatorships with whom we have relatively close relations.

But I think also there is another notion, another objective, that may be in the process of being brushed aside. If so, it is an extremely dangerous development. Half the American people can no longer remember World War II, and fewer than that can remember the events which led up to World War II. I am concerned that the great central question we all faced in 1945—How do we organize a durable peace?—is being forgotten.

If this is now true, I cannot underline too much the dangers involved. It is not just a matter of recalling the terrible price that was paid in the years 1939-45 because the governments of the preceding era proved themselves incapable of organizing, or unwilling to organize, a peace. Looking toward the future, it is literally true that the survival of man may be at stake. When one thinks of the thousands upon thousands of nuclear warheads in existence, the necessity of organizing a durable peace cannot be forgotten, cannot be overlooked. So, I believe there is a lot of work to be done by all of us in trying to get at some of the essentials of international organization and international survival.

A second general range of suggestions has to do with dealing with the sheer complexity in international affairs. For example, when a pilot takes off in his aircraft, particularly if he has a complex, modern aircraft, he has a very long checklist. It is now so long it is kept rolled up in a cylinder, and the crew goes through that checklist, asking themselves dozens upon dozens of questions before they take the plane off the ground. Now, what kind of a checklist should we go through before we take off on a policy? I have tried to do some work on that myself here in the Department. The list of questions, and the list of secondary questions, for each important policy matter is very long, and has in it almost an infin-

11

ity of elements. Yet, if major factors are omitted in making the decision, something is very likely to go wrong.

There is a very great difference between an opinion and a decision. One does not have to discount opinion to recognize that difference. And under our system people are entitled to have an opinion, for good reasons or bad reasons or no reasons at all. They are entitled to postpone having an opinion. They are entitled to change their opinion overnight. For the most part, those who live on opinions or can afford to have only opinions very seldom have to live with the results of their conclusions.

Decisions are quite another matter. In the first place they cannot be postponed, because a postponement is in itself a decision. Any policy officer who puts on his hat and goes home makes some decisions by not doing something else that day, by putting it off until tomorrow. We are trying to find ways to be conscious of the decisions we are making, even in the process of not making them.

Decisions have to take into account all the factors that seem to have a bearing on the issue to be decided. The problem of the fatal flaw for the decision maker is a very serious problem, so that a comprehensive view of the situation about which a decision is being made is vitally important if wisdom is to have a chance to play its role. And we have perhaps not given enough attention to this problem. It is something of a habit for purposes of analysis and study to extract particular elements and study those. But, in the great processes of politics, it is very hard to extract one or two or three elements, because then other factors are not the same. Every question is a part of a context. And we have the unhappy situation that almost every important question merges into almost every other important question. It is difficult to solve them all at once, but it is also difficult to solve one of them outside the context in which it arises.

There is another field concerned with policy and planning that is perhaps peculiarly the responsibility of the universities. Policy is, by and large, dealing with the future. Our chief function in the Department of State is to try to bring about one kind of future rather than another kind of future, but there are some problems in trying to pierce the fog of the future and make a little more sense rather than a little less sense out of unfolding events. And again, pace is very important, and sometimes—very often—we think about the social, the political, the humanistic aspects of developments too late. Research laboratories are hurling us into the future at a breathtaking pace, and I wonder if we have enough reflection from the social sciences and the humanities about the human implications of what is happening in these laboratories. I am not sure that we do.

I remember in the early fifties that I talked to some friends in some universities about the need for preparatory work on the law and politics of outer space. My proposal was met with colossal indifference! One very distinguished professor, internationally known, said at that time that "the future is not the business of the university." But at that very moment the laboratories at his own university were hurling us into it. So, when Sputnik went up, there was a great rush to enter the space race, and to begin to think about the law and politics of outer space. Now, ten years after Sputnik, we have succeeded in concluding a very important treaty on outer space. The timing is not too bad, but it was relatively a simple matter to accomplish because space is so difficult that there was not a great deal of activity in it, and space is so remote that it has not engaged the turmoils and the jealousies and the rivalries that exist here on the face of the Earth.

There are also other things we must soon confront, for example, weather modification. This new capability is going to be with us within a decade—important capabilities for modifying weather, a hundred times more complex, quarrelsome, and competitive, than outer space. I just wonder who in the United States is giving some thought to the law and politics of weather modification, because there lies great capability not only for good but also for causing wars. And it will take all the wit we can pull together to make some sense out of this new capability which is coming relatively fast.

The utilization of the resources of the open seas is another development that perhaps needs more attention, though it has been getting some. Are we going to enter a period in which rivalry for the control of open ocean is going to be comparable to the rush for control of land areas in the eighteenth and nineteenth centuries? There are very great problems involved in matters of this sort.

I mention these concerns not in terms of complaint, but to say to the academic community that, whether anyone wants it or not, the expansion of human knowledge is moving very fast, particularly the expansion of scientific knowledge, and, therefore, there is a responsibility to think about the other aspects—the human, the political, the legal—of the new world that is opening in front of us.

These are some of the areas in which we need all the help we can get from the universities. We in government would like to be able to be of help to the academic community but stay out of its way at the same time, so that government does not intrude in the wrong way into the university field. But we continue to need from the university not only ideas and trained people, but also the tremendous contribution that this community continues to make to

13

the solidarity of man. We are going to come to a point where those things that are common to *homo sapiens* are going to be increasingly important, and the issues that divide are going to be less important. I believe there is room for substantially greater initiative in international affairs to discover those things which have nothing to do with ideology or national frontiers, those things in which all men have a deep common interest. There is no such thing as a Communist wheat rust or a Capitalist potato blight. Food problems will soon be so serious that we ought to find some way to bring the human race to address itself to them without regard to ideology. Little by little those great common interests may put a restraining hand on the more violent nature of man and give us a chance to build some peace.

Now I end where I began with the universities' contribution to the great problem of building an enduring peace, which is the most critical problem of all. I hope that all of us, in government and outside, can find ways to think harder about it, and perhaps find ways to do more about it, because the stakes could not be higher.

Government and Universities:
The Evolving Relationship

One of the pleasantest parts of my job here in the Department of State is that I so often have official reasons for meeting with members of the same academic club I have belonged to. Since coming to Washington I have had some of my most important and educational discussions, in fact, with several members of the Columbia faculty. It is a special pleasure for me to have the opportunity which this seminar provides for such a discussion.

Charles Frankel

What I should like to do now is look beyond the past year or eighteen months, during which important government initiatives have been launched, and ask more long-term questions. Where do the universities stand and where does government stand with respect to one another and to the common problem they share of doing business with one another?

If we look at this problem, I think we cannot fail to see that it is considerably confused. Old, indeed ancient, misconceptions still prevail that make discussion of it difficult. Let me talk first, therefore, about the general context of our discussion—about premises that may not rise to the surface as early as they should unless I bring them to the surface here at the outset.

It is common today to put the problem of the American university in relation to government in rather melodramatic terms. The question is sometimes put: Should universities be useful, or should they retain their classic identity and integrity? Or, to put the question in more personal terms, should professors corrupt themselves and enter government for the sake of influence and power, or should they remain pure but poor, superior but alienated?

I think this is a false dichotomy—false both historically and intellectually. There has never been a time when universities and learning have been useless. There has never been a time when any society regarded universities and learning as useless, or when universities have been separated or alien from the society around them. What has changed is the conception of what usefulness is. What has changed is the conception of the relationship between

15

the learned community and the rest of society that ought to prevail.

In the Middle Ages the monastic ideal of learning held that the learned man should indeed be in retreat. The learned man represented an effort to maintain an eternal point of view, an intellectual and moral commitment that would be at odds with the corruption, the despair, the pure temporality of his society. But the fulfillment of this obligation was a service to society. It was a way to maintain in one form a visible image of the City of God. It reminded society of what was ultimately of value, of what was really useful.

The humanist ideal, which secularized this concept, was not dissimilar. Universities should represent, this ideal maintained, the finer things of life, not because the finer things of life are useless, but because they are useful. And certainly universities, in the day when class distinctions were stronger and firmer than they are today, represented a class idea, the perpetuation of an aristocratic code and a traditional body of wisdom—or, if you will, folklore—around which the prevailing class distinctions turned and through which they were sanctioned.

It is these notions of utility that are now being changed—not the idea that universities should be useful. The sources of this change lie in social changes, changes with respect to which our educational philosophy has still to wrestle. The basic changes lie in the rationalizing of work and of the economy. Increasingly, ordinary routines of work depend not on inherited traditions, but on deliberate decisions based upon knowledge—or, at any rate, on what is alleged to be knowledge. Government, too, is being rationalized. I don't know whether it is being made more intelligent, but more and more of government is being carried on by people who are the expositors of certain specialized intellectual disciplines, and who are not regarded simply as the exponents of a body of general wisdom or gentlemanly intelligence.

What has happened, in sum, is that there is emerging a new relationship in our world between traditional skills and erudition, and new and explicit skills—skills you can write down in a book and pass on in texts, changing skills that have to be remade every decade in the light of new problems and new knowledge. These changing skills have largely replaced the old skills that belonged to the crafts and to the body of knowledge—the "mystery"—that you had to master in order to qualify for a guild. Moreover, formal book learning of some sort has become an antecedent condition for carrying on an increasing number of ordinary activities. The number of activities that can be carried on in a developed technical society without much formal education is rapidly diminishing.

Another factor bears even more pointedly on traditional distinctions between theoretical and practical forms of learning and education. There has been a revolution within the community of learning itself. The notion of what it means to be learned has changed. The growth of science has changed the ideal of knowledge itself because it has produced the conception of experimental knowledge. It has introduced the conception of knowledge tested in some form of action or active observation. In consequence, our universities have changed, physically and visibly. There are more and more buildings on every campus that look like industrial buildings. This is not an accident, and it does not mean that universities are being corrupted. It simply means that many of the university's activities are becoming more and more similar to activities going on in industrial establishments. But these activities remain intellectual. Indeed, if we talk about the industrialization of the university, we also ought to talk about the intellectualization of industry.

I need not dwell on any of these points; they are all well known to you. They provide the landscape on which universities and government must work out their relationships. What are the dangers these new facts create? One danger is the impulse to resist, the impulse to keep things simple, the impulse to say that the older ideals of learning define the function and vocation of a modern university. If we take this point of view, we do so, I think, at the price of destroying what must now be accepted as valid knowledge and valid elements in the process of disciplined inquiry and education. A reverse danger is to idolize technique and the latest methodology. The machinery of inquiry can be so large and imposing that the fact that it is a means to an end can be easily overlooked. And equally dangerous is the allied tendency to speak in pious but undefined terms about service to something encompassing called "the community" or "the nation."

It has always been the function of the university, and of learned men, to comment on the passing moment from the standpoint of standards and insights that transcend the passing moment. It has always been the function of the best universities and the best intellectuals to serve as guides and critics for their societies—to help in the selection of purposes and ends. This means that they have not simply offered or sold their services. They have not simply contributed to the power and comfort of their society. They have made their society at times more uncomfortable. They have questioned the rationale and the uses of its power. They have not

17

merely provided techniques for solving problems other people have formulated.

In the last ten or fifteen years, universities have probably succumbed too often to the temptation to be odd jobbers in the American community. Neither on the side of the universities nor on that of government, have we really tried to lay down ground rules for a relationship between the nation and the universities that would permit the universities to do the things they can do best in their own best terms. And as a result, we face perhaps the greatest of all dangers, which is simply the fuzzing of all the rules. Because the relationship between education and the rest of the nation has become so pervasive and so encircling, because government and universities touch one another at so many points and overlap at so many points, because there is a steady overlapping and interchanging of roles, we need to be very sharp about the definition of roles. This necessary job of definition has not been done. There has been vagueness about the basic rules of the game.

My own thoughts about such basic rules are, I confess, neither very new nor very complicated. Basically, it seems to me that Rule Number One has to be that universities are instruments for the criticism of ends as well as for the development of instrumentalities and means, and they must therefore maintain full intellectual independence and autonomy. This means more than that our society should continue to safeguard the principles of academic freedom. The threat of government control has to be guarded against. But the significant threat is not palpable control. The significant threat is the impalpable influence of government. The resources of government are so great that universities in their growth and in their direction may lose the power or the will to be self-determining. They can allow central power to determine the direction of their own work, of their own growth and development. If this happens, no one will be better off. The main burden in preventing it lies with university people themselves.

This leads to Rule Two—that government should increasingly attempt to get *behind* the educational community, to strengthen its resources, to stimulate and encourage its participation in domestic as in international affairs. But government, at the same time, should try to get out of the middle of the operation, to get behind the operation and stay out of the middle. It must find ways to support universities so that they can do on their own what they can do best.

The third rule is to recognize that education has its own character and function. When institutions are used for purposes other than education, they do the job badly, and the special purposes they can and must serve are lost. There is a temptation in every society, and there is in ours, to use education and culture for purely technical purposes, or for propagandistic purposes, or if I may say so to this audience, for "high-ideal" political purposes. I am regularly surprised that, at meetings I attend, the scholars always want to talk about the contribution of their discipline to international peace, while I always want to talk to them about what the State Department or the government can do to help them in the pursuit of their own disciplines, within and across the borders of our country. I think this is a problem to which Aristotle's wisdom applies: he remarked in his *Ethics*, as you will recall, that no man is happy if he aims directly at finding happiness. Happiness, as he said, is a by-product of other activities. I have no doubt that if educators and universities do what they can do in their own proper terms, they will contribute to international peace as a by-product. I do not say that they should not think or talk about international peace. Neither do I say that they trespass into territory they should avoid when they protest the actions of their government in foreign affairs. I merely express the hope they do not sacrifice their own special purposes while talking about exciting designs for international peace.

Against that background it may be easier to see the reasons for programs the Federal Government has been developing over the last eighteen months. It is against this background that the International Education Act of 1966 was passed by the Congress. Its purpose is to give universities long-term power to establish or develop programs of international studies useful to their own educational purposes.

Secondly, it is against this background that there is emerging a new element in foreign policy. Much has been done in the last eighteen months by the government to encourage the free international movement of intellectuals, scholars, and students. Regulations have been simplified and unnecessary restrictions removed so that people can come to our country more easily. Further, the exchange programs that we have developed over the last twenty years are being converted to new and more ambitious purposes. Twenty years ago they were aimed, quite properly, at the exchange of individuals and at broadening the horizons of individuals. Now we see them in a somewhat larger perspective. Their old function remains, but we also are attempting to use these exchanges more deliberately to help create a kind of institutional interdependence across the borders—a kind of organized and planned educational interdependence—in the interest of learning and education and,

19

indeed, in the interests of peace and understanding. Our programs are now being more systematically planned from this point of view. Broadly, we are trying to create within the Department of State and within the government as a whole a more coordinated approach so that we can test these exchanges not only from the point of view of their value to individuals, but also from the point of view of their capacity for strengthening national and international institutions for cooperative educational purposes.

All this seems to me to call for some further steps—steps on the academic side and steps on the government's side. I think the universities and the learned societies need really to think about a new educational policy, a new shape for the life of the professor or intellectual. Today, participation in international affairs or international scholarship continues to be regarded, to speak in metaphorical terms, largely as a sabbatical-year affair. Although more and more professors and educators are engaged in international exchanges of one sort or another, these engagements are still regarded as intermissions in the intellectual's career. Administrators tend to regard them as somewhat troublesome. Departments tend to regard them as interruptions in the normal schedules of their members.

Membership in the academic community now implies that a man will find himself drawn increasingly over the years into the international scholarly community. Fifty years ago, the university community had to settle some very basic problems about tenure, retirement rights, and the like. Today, I think, the university has a new set of problems which it will have to settle in a similar way. What shall be regarded as normal for a university career? What arrangements shall a university make to take these facts into account? How shall teaching be remade? How shall the ideals of research and scholarship be redefined so that we measure success and utility in the terms that are appropriate for our day?

I am not nearly so disturbed by the drain of academics from the universities—though it is disturbing—as I am by the failure to clarify the terms in which such phenomena can be discussed. I think this is very much the business of the university community and it is unfinished business. Once the universities have decided how they are going to operate in these fields, government can then work out with the universities mutually satisfactory mechanisms.

It is in these terms that I hope we can continue to work in international education. From this point of view, we have made in my Bureau, a deliberate effort to bring working scholars actively into our planning processes. And we are also going to push ahead with the task of implementing the legislation we now have—

legislation which is aimed at giving government the long-term power to accommodate itself to the changes in the university scene, and to helping universities to be what they should be in the government's own interest—the masters of their own destiny.

Government, the Universities, and International Affairs:
The Common Responsibilities

**C. W.
de Kiewiet**

President Johnson's Smithsonian speech, and the legislation which promises substantial support for the role of the universities in the international field, can be a watershed. The impact upon the universities may be comparable, ten or fifteen years hence, with some of the great changes wrought by federal support for the sciences. The gate has been opened to bringing the American university much closer to the national interest in its foreign policy.

In domestic and now prospectively in international matters the university system of the United States has become vital to the effectiveness of the country to a degree that would have sounded inflated and unnatural a generation ago. The closeness of the American university to the life and work of its environment has long distinguished it from other university systems. But today there is a further road to be traveled which is scarcely mapped, and there are new and greater tasks, foreign and domestic, to be shouldered.

The great themes and preoccupations of American foreign policy are two in number. They can be likened to two trunks, growing out of many roots, and spreading into many branches. The first is the prevention of World War III. The second is success in helping to fill the vacuums or insufficiencies of stability, prosperity, health, and modern competence in what today are gently called the developing countries. These are twin trunks, but not identical. Each has its own being, its own problems, and its own requirements. Their contemporaneity and the undoubted overlapping and joining of many issues still do not warrant the very common assumption that their meaning in American foreign policy comes from the Cold War and the great strains between world powers. What is partly true is not wholly true. Otherwise the absurd and dangerous conclusion would be reached that a settlement between the world powers would in the same degree reduce the urgency or the problems of the developing countries of Africa, Asia, and Latin America.

The awful need to prevent World War III produces a fear of any war (at all) as the possible trigger of total disaster. The knowledge, however, that the world is dealing with two major issues, rather than one, suggests that the avoidance of all conflict is not a possibility. One cannot wishfully dismiss real problems by putting forth unreal answers. In 1945 nothing was more certain than a long generation of turbulent transition from an old order to a new. For a country that stepped right out of isolationism into global conflict in 1941, the hardest lesson has been to learn to live with problems that are dangerous, with violence that may erupt anywhere, and uncertainties that confuse its thought.

This paper is principally concerned with the second major preoccupation of American foreign policy, which is the filling of the voids, vacuums, and insufficiencies of the new world brought into being by the passing of the empires of the nineteenth century. This role is of deep interest to the university world.

A minor theologian in the Middle Ages once pointed to God's wise husbandry in letting the rain fall on the fertile valleys and plains rather than on the desert where it would be wasted. In the twentieth century this distinction is still with us. The right men, usually white, who live in the right places, mostly Europe and North America, do the right things, mostly profitable. Much of the rest of the world endures infertility, disease, ignorance, and poverty. These are some of the vacuums which we can no longer justify theologically, and which we leave unfilled at our own peril. These vacuums are accompanied by voids in political power, domestic stability, financial resources, and a fair prospect for the future.

Political independence of new nations is a legal fact. But it is not yet given full substance by satisfactions which they can provide for themselves. Political independence is qualified by an uncorrected dependence upon others. This anomaly is so dangerous that it justifies the name of a distinct major crisis.

It is now clearer than it could have been even a few years ago that the achievement of political independence was a remarkably incomplete consummation. The admiration for the calm and usually amicable character of the transformation of the nineteenth century colonial systems must be more restrained. There did seem something miraculous that great empires could end without shaking the world. From India in 1947 to Guyana in 1966 the world seemed almost unbelievably fortunate in not suffering the havoc of colonial wars and insurrection. Algeria and French Indo-China were exceptions that tested the rule. One felt a debt of historic gratitude to the United Kingdom and France in particular for

23

sparing the world the bloodshed and the enduring rancors that are caused by revolution.

The feeling of admiration and the sense of debt still have merit. But they apply mostly to the legal and constitutional settlements. We were guilty of reading too much of the history of the past into the history of the present, of invoking the doctrines of Europe and America in dealing with Africa and Asia. Americans read far too much of their own revolution into the independence movement in the postwar world.

What Charles de Gaulle calls the Anglo-Saxon mind places the highest value on the phenomenon of constitution making. Successful constitutions were amongst the great achievements of the United States, Great Britain, and the major nineteenth century colonies of settlement. These constitutions were consummations of considerable past development, and therefore good foundations for further development. The attitude of enthusiasm and relief over the paper wording of the constitutions of the twentieth century assumed that the history of the eighteenth and nineteenth centuries would happily repeat itself in the twentieth century.

Because we have considerably overestimated the achievement of the first step in the process of decolonialization, we have also underestimated the further steps needed to carry the process towards maturity. One conclusion is especially important. There is no assurance after all that the world has miraculously been spared the storm and stress of the passing of historic empires. At worst the storm and stress could still break over us.

In seeking to understand the forces with which the United States must deal, we must recognize that this second great preoccupation of American foreign policy is really much greater than the crisis of the breakdown of the nineteenth century imperialism. Both chronology and geography must be extended in order to include the total period of imperial and colonial activity since the sixteenth century, and to include all the parts of the world affected by that activity. The mid-twentieth century is faced with a reckoning of the human costs of four centuries of history. There is therefore a continuity and a basic identity between the historically submerged groups and populations of the Americas, North and South, and those of Africa and much of Asia. The great domestic American crisis over the status of the Negro is indissolubly part of the international crisis. Each influences the other, and both share similar causes. It is only by recognizing this wider context of chronology and geography that we can measure the gravity of the world situation, and see the inextricable character of American involvement. About this involvement, there is nothing peripheral or external or temporary.

The conquered and dispossessed of four centuries are rewriting their own history. The Western world has lost its monopoly over the interpretation of the colonial and imperial era. This is an event of far greater moment than the overwhelming of the Catholic interpretation of the expansion of Europe by the historiography of the Protestant and commercial nations. It is an intellectual event, but it is even more meaningful in its dynamic quality, its capacity of becoming a powerful force in the shaping of individual nations and the relations between them.

The American Revolution was accomplished by, indeed preceded by, an informed and assertive political debate. We have failed to notice that the thinkers of the new nations, whether lowly or gifted, are a full generation and more slower in their emergence than the intellectuals of the American eighteenth century. Their emergence will not be simply a literary accomplishment. Within the civil rights movement in the United States the phenomenon of Negro slavery, deprivation, and secondariness is being intensely reviewed. It is being reviewed in two forms, or perhaps according to two methods. Martin Luther King and his followers are interpreting the Negro past as Americans, albeit Negro Americans. In thought, word and deed they are drawing heavily and authentically on the Christian ethic, on the classic concepts of Western politics and jurisprudence. But there are others who are conducting their reviews of the race as Negroes with much less respect for or reliance upon established doctrine. From their interpretation they derive the deepest sense of grievance, feel a wider chasm between themselves and the rest of the nation, and above all feel compelled to seek remedy along paths of violence and insurrection rather than of constitutional and legal redress.

These thoughts are not advanced as either a profound or precise analysis of the complex civil rights crisis, but for two other important reasons. The first is to give a domestic illustration of developments to be watched for abroad, especially in Africa. The second is to indicate the acute interest which the American student can and must take in the autonomous review by the students of the new emerging world of the colonial era and its aftermath.

At the moment it seems acceptable to say that the spokesmen and leaders of the emergent societies draw on an ethic and on concepts that can readily be found in the environment of British, French and American universities. This is a condition of capital significance. One can readily discern the rewards that would flow from a continuous, active, and cooperative relationship between the intellectual and university communities of the new nations and the old. This language does not mean a more subtle projection

25

of an earlier monopoly of analysis and interpretation. It means a studious, laborious, and creative inquiry into the crisis of the areas of vacuum and insufficiency, into its causes, its manifestations, and its requirements. If this statement is acceptable, we obviously stand before a most comprehensive task of adjustment and appraisal in the university curriculum and research dealing with foreign affairs. This would deal with guiding ideas, methods, interdisciplinary relationships, and new categories of knowledge.

If the course of international events, and our national handling of them, serve to intensify frustrations and multiply disappointments, if an honest community of interest cannot be developed, we must prepare ourselves for an interpretation of the African, Asian, and Latin American past and present written in terms of rejection, resentment, and the deepest rancor. The lesson of Kwame Nkrumah points to more than the evils of demagoguery, peculation, and megalomania. His eclipse should not blind us to the fact that he was expressing some of the radicalism and violence of the traditional revolutionary against the *ancien regime*. His folly and excess were obvious, but he can yet represent an anticipation of a mental radicalism and a physical uprising against arrangements, relationships, and the ideas that are too obviously taken for granted if we study the trend in our assistance programs.

The downward trend in assistance programs is in part caused by a failure to see the close relationship between domestic and international issues, in part also by the mistake of regarding foreign aid too much as a maneuver or episode in the Cold War. One discerns also a neo-isolationism whose followers would not object to seeing most of the new African and Asian states drift into the company of the Latin American states, politically free, but in a secondary and satellite relationship to the wealthy metropolitan world. It is most doubtful that the twentieth century will agree to endure quietly what the nineteenth century endured.

In the area of vacuums, voids and insufficiencies, hopes too long deferred, frustrations too long evident, and satisfactions too long withheld could even bring about a violent fusion of the twin issues of American foreign policy. Misconception and complacency may turn the struggle of the new nations to fill the vacuum of power and satisfactions into radical channels. New experiments, new methods of organizing society, new imports of power and competence, altogether would constitute a grim alteration in the political and economic shape of the world. If there is a Communist challenge, this is it.

African and Asian states are in no danger of a brutal reimposition of former colonial regimes. But they still face two forms of dependence or secondariness. An aggressive African mind might call the first residual or crypto-colonialism and the second neocolonialism. The first is the incompleteness and the underdevelopment which have already been described. The second is, or could be, a neocolonialism of a very modern and special nature. It could develop with African, Asian, and Latin American consent, on the invitation of indigenous governments, as a new radical, and presumably Communist inspired, experiment in international collaboration in order to hasten change, and more readily fill the vacuums of power and satisfaction.

With these matters the American university community has an intellectual concern, an organizational concern, and an operational concern. The first concern is with scholarship, research, analysis, and the creation of guiding concepts. The second concern is with the manner in which scholars and their institutions work with government in the use of the support now being promised. The third concern is with activities and responsibilities of universities in the international field, and especially in the countries of limited development.

The United States travels a stormy course with inadequate bearings. Its conceptual map of the world requires revision. One can speak, with a French twist to the phrase, of an American crisis of consciousness or conception of the modern world. We share these lacks with every other nation, but in a more urgent and comprehensive form, simply because we are more deeply and dangerously involved. As a defeated and shattered nation Japan had to rebuild its conceptual map of the world. President de Gaulle began to do so for France visibly and dramatically during the Algerian insurrection. The British nation is still laboriously and anxiously redrawing its own map and identifying its most realistic and dignified place within it. The equivalent American task is far greater and most incomplete.

As a world power the United States is deprived of the simple formulas of the day when it was possible to conduct foreign policy by slogan. That day, not surprisingly, was a torpid and uncreative period in American scholarship in international affairs. Today foreign policy has become extraordinarily intricate. In their fullness the problems of foreign relations have lost any obviousness or easiness of comprehension. The resources of knowledge and the degrees of practical acquaintance that are required put a value on detailed expertness and critical analytical judgment as never before. While government in the strict sense is the creator of policies, while it must make choices and secure accommodations that are the most promising for the interests of the country, these tasks are

27

not satisfied by a delegation to those in authority alone. The process of policy making must involve acceptance by trained professional intellectuals of a vast task of examination, of thought, and of clarification. It is a labor of study, assessment, and review that can never be complete, can never be perfect, and can never be laid down. The obvious university share of this process will call for staff, time, and programs which at the moment it does not sufficiently command.

This university responsibility has important quantitative and important qualitative connotations. The postwar world has seen a multiplication of points of independent action and decision, and therefore a multiplication of areas and issues capable of throwing up difficult problems. They are of an economic character, of a demographic character, of a political character, of a military character. Southeast Asia, the Middle East, North Africa, black Africa, southern Africa are items in a longer catalog of areas of imbalance and controversy that no longer can be easily controlled from the dominant metropolitan centers of the nineteenth century. Only a generation ago the study of Great Britain or France provided guidelines to understanding the much larger areas that depended on them, and could be influenced by them.

In their swift succession the distinctness of problems and the vividness of crises dissolve into a blur. The public state of mind is rather one of uneasiness and anxiety than of clear comprehension. The result is sometimes a shrugging surrender of thought and decision, or a stridency of protest based more on panic than knowledge. Reporters and commentators labor daily to explain and clarify the issues of international relations. Probably no country is better served. Yet all of their efforts are grossly inadequate to the volume of information to be grasped, to the complexity of problems, to the intricacy of their relationships. The powers of thought and analysis lag behind the heaving mass of fact and of happening. There is not too much exaggeration in the remark that every time a new country achieves independence, there is created a new branch of study for which there must be responsibility somewhere in our universities. If there is statesmanship in the President's plans, and wisdom in their administration, the enhancement of such academic competence is one important goal.

There would be exaggeration in any conclusion that an increase in the number of individual specialists in a greater series of separate fields and subjects would satisfy the qualitative aspect of increased university responsibility in international relations. The moment has come to open again with fresh urgency the debate of twenty years ago between disciplinary specialization and interdisciplinary competence as means of grasping and making available the concepts that may guide national policy. At that time the battle was lost to the traditional disciplinarians. Only a few years ago a study revealed the astonishing fact that only one of several ambitious African studies centers was genuinely interdisciplinary in character. A fresh debate would be essential if important federal funds are to attain their purpose. Wherever scholars try today to establish the relevance of their information to some practical action, they unfailingly recognize their dependence upon an interdisciplinary synthesis of information, or more clearly upon an arrangement of knowledge in categories that transcend the conventional categories. Interdisciplinarians in manpower planning, education, history, have already emerged as pioneers of curricular changes that would be the essential creative response of universities to the initiative which national legislation is extending to them.

The qualitative connotation of the responsibility of higher learning in the life of the nation includes the great international issues but goes far beyond and above them. Phrases like a conceptual map of the modern world, or the crisis of American consciousness of the world, depend for their meaning on the fact that mankind seems to be undergoing one of those epochal transformations that mark the close of one age and the arrival of another. Scientific epithets like nuclear age and space age fall short of adequate description. In the lifetime of men still young, born during the Great Depression, have come changes with a speed, an intensity, a greatness of promise and an awfulness of menace, that form one of the authentic watersheds of all human history. Greatly multiplied, enormously more intense, breathlessly speeded up, it is the crisis which Rome the city endured when it became Rome the empire, or more nearly the crisis which Europe endured when it had to understand and absorb the Protestant revolution, the use of scientific inquiry, the beginnings of capitalism, the nation state, and the voyages of exploration, with the consequent bursting of the narrow mental and physical context of the Middle Ages.

These words can only begin to measure the tasks that face the inquiring mind, or to indicate how much the ranks of scholarship must be expanded. The administration in Washington has clearly seen this need. It has taken a long step further in a process which began with the Morrill Act. In some ways recent legislation is one of the most notable and explicit acts of recognition of the nation's deep dependence on its universities. One must sympathize with President Johnson's reported bewilderment at the low level of enthusiasm shown by the academic community for an historic act of confidence. The university mind seems to have missed the combination of deference and compliment in the President's appeals for fresh thought on the problems of the nation, possibly because of their unbookish wording. Men who have spent their lives within universities know that the search for truth does not always lead to tolerance and understanding. It sometimes breeds a foggy sacerdotalism which is intolerant and even cruel. Yet those who live within universities also know that there is an inborn statesmanship that will avail itself of the latest challenge and the latest opportunity.

We are certainly beholding an advanced stage in the century-long movement of the American university into a deeper relationship with its own society. The President's attitude recognizes and facilitates a transformation that was already powerfully in motion. This transformation is more than a growth in size, in the number of institutions, enrollments, or an expansion of strictly traditional functions.

The explosion of knowledge is a familiar phrase. Robert Oppenheimer gave it a mathematical twist by saying that man's knowledge doubles every decade. A statistical version declares that there are more scientists at work in this generation than have lived and worked since ancient Greece. But these scientific equations go no further in describing what is happening than the equivalent statement that university libraries are expanding at a geometric rate. The force of the explosion of knowledge is more concretely evident in the fact that the explosion is equally great in the practical applications of knowledge, and in the consequent phenomenon that the traditional boundaries of the university world have been transgressed, fissured, and blurred.

The fund raising speeches of university presidents always proclaim the dependence of society upon universities for power, progress, and prosperity. The mendicant pronouncements of the presidents are confirmed by the scientific thought of the professors. Theodore Schultz proved that education, capital, and labor were the three equal pillars on which a modern nation held itself aloft. Recently, the most remarkable demonstration has come from the less tutored environments of the new countries. Somewhat unexpectedly the developing nations are proving to be a laboratory in which the role of the university as a principal and vital instrument in building a nation has been most clearly apparent. It became apparent in controversy between young universities and young governments. It is difficult to condone the actions of Kwame Nkrumah at the University of Ghana, or of the University Council at the University of Lagos, or more recently Julius Nyerere's emotional expulsion of almost the entire Tanzanian student body at Dar es Salaam. Yet one fact emerges with the sharpest clarity. A university is invested with a very real and a very direct responsibility in the task of building new nations, or sustaining the progress of a mature nation. Wherever there is failure to recognize this responsibility, there is also the tragedy of misunderstanding and the confusion of controversy. When misunderstanding and controversy turn to anger, there is distress and punishment for both sides.

Fundamental to an understanding of the closer movement of the university to the life of practical action are certain changes in the nature and purpose of scholarship and research. There has come about a blurring, some would say a disappearance, of the dogmatic distinctions between pure research and applied research, between thought and consequent action or use, between principle and practice. In a manner not coarse or expedient, but sophisticated and essential, there has come about the conquest of the spirit of the entire university by the original genius of the land grant college. In the language of Benedetto Croce thought is the thought of action, and action is the action of thought. The Manhattan Project of World War II was the first definitive demonstration of an immediate and inseparable collaboration between theory and application, between the laboratory and factory. There is a fusion today between technology and science, an interpenetration of each by the other, that makes nonsense of the traditional separation between the ivory tower and the practical world. What the Manhattan Project began has been carried spectacularly forward by the compelling requirements of the nuclear and space age. We have experienced the collapse of what Professor Medawar called the Anglo-Saxon obsession with a complete intellectual and methodological distinction between pure and applied thought. One can come to the same conclusion in chronological or temporal terms. The condition of the modern world, the problems of modern society, and the relations between nations compel the promptest closing of the gap in time or progression between knowledge expressed in theoretical shape, and knowledge in its dynamic form. One might speak of the modern mobilization of knowledge, or, a little less safely, of the conversion of mass into energy, or its academic inertness into social activity.

One meets with diminishing objections when applying these arguments to science, medicine, or engineering. They may still sound strange and forced when applied, as they now must be, to the relations between men and nations. George Harrar made this wider and equally urgent application plain in a commencement

31

address at Emory University. Overpopulation in the modern world, planless urbanization, explosive racial prejudice, pollution of air and water, deteriorating social mores, the hunger of scores of nations for modern existence, are samples of peremptory problems that call for the same close collaboration between men of thought and men of action. President Johnson's request for new ideas was unfairly made to appear the pathetic mark of an unacademic mind shopping for ideas which it could not generate itself. A fairer view recognizes that the President was pointing to the need to narrow and reduce the gaps between thought and practice, the delays between discovery and innovation. He stood on an advanced frontier of the academic movement by going beyond the material and technical exigencies of defense and space exploration. The great domestic and international crises were discernibly the main focus of his attention. Thus one can speak of an invitation to the total university community to enter more fully, more directly, more constructively into the great issues of the nation.

Before returning to the university and international relations, a brief explanation of the transgression or blurring of university boundaries will be useful. Methods and instruments born within the university have taken root in industry, commerce, and government. The great industries and major departments of government eagerly recruit the experts working within the universities, or borrow them as advisers and consultants. Their laboratories and specialized training programs are planned adaptations of the arrangements and atmosphere of the university. There is a brisk and constant movement of men of specialized talent to and fro between the university and industry, commerce, diplomacy, and government. Although the university retains its specific traditional functions, a situation now exists comparable to that described by Professor Galbraith in discussing the relations between industry and government. Much of the traditional frontier between private industry and government has been eroded. The enormously costly and complicated undertakings in space science, communications, and national defense make meaningless many of the doctrines of the free market or of the essential separateness between the private and public sectors. Problems of planning, financing, and decision making have compelled an intimacy of cooperation without which these problems cannot find a successful solution. This situation is now developing in higher education. The great issues in domestic and foreign policy make most palpably urgent the development of adequate instruments and practices of consultation, communication, and cooperation. There is required what Professor Harbison terms a strategy in the broad relationship between government and higher education, and very especially a strategy in specific projects and areas of common effort. This necessary frontier of discourse and effort is seriously in need of fresh understandings, arrangements, and procedures. To make one clear and specific contribution, there can be no question at all about the immediate need of giving greater coherence and "planfulness" to the role of government and university in their assistance to developing countries.

One must, quite bluntly if necessary, turn aside the conventional suspicion that academic freedom and a constructive awareness of social needs, especially when revealed in government policy, are incompatible. It is quite all right to give a precautionary flap to the old flag, in case it may be needed, as long as we see realistically and objectively that the great growth in university effectiveness in this generation has depended upon the intelligent willingness of the great public and private agencies to turn to the universities for assistance.

On the assumption that support for international studies and activities will be provided, some important questions must be asked. With what insights and resoluteness will these new resources be administered? What safeguards will there be that they will not be diluted in university and college budgets under some dull and safe formula of evenhandedness? An uninspired apportionment through bureaucratic timidity, or largesse through political pressure are ever present dangers. These prospective resources can be an historic and creative force in the nature and structure of American higher education. They are an investment that can buy special and desirable things. The best of our foundations provide some valuable guidelines.

The best of American foundations are envied by foreign observers for more than their wealth. They have learned that their highest mandate is to stimulate needed change, to look for opportunities on the frontiers of knowledge and action. Indeed a part of the best innovative academic leadership has passed to the foundations. The very field of our present concern would not be so promising, had it not been for the deliberate choice by the major foundations to promote its interests. At their best the foundations have specialized in the recognition of frontiers, in the anticipation of major needs, in the negotiation of critical change, and in the discovery of new instruments and procedures. To have these skills, this innovative temper, at the point of exchange and cooperation between government and universities is a goal worthy of the best thought and effort.

The logic of the magnitude and inescapable nature of international issues leads directly to two conclusions. First, there is a need for an increased dimension of university concern and activity. The second conclusion is that this concern and this activity cannot be short in duration or unplanned in application.

There has been an understandable miscalculation at home and abroad about the effort and time needed to provide developing countries with assistance. Legislators do not like indeterminate financial commitments. Yet terminal appropriations encourage fragmented undertakings, limit imagination, discourage foresight, and substitute a short-range expediency for strategic planning. The new leaders in the new countries miscalculated because they were, and still have to be, men in a hurry. What the past had taken or deferred over centuries, the present is asked to restore or provide in decades. In the language of American history they have insisted on completely revising Turner's thesis of frontier development. There is no consent in the mind of Kenyatta or Kaunda to the idea of societies growing through the patient labor of individual men who overcome obstacles by trial and error, slowly accumulating their own capital, learning their own science, and devising their own technology. The pioneers of today are educators, scientists, engineers, doctors, trained officials, and managers. The place of the covered wagon and the log house is taken by the university. Europe's ancient universities were centuries old before they began to acquire the plant, staff, and curriculum which the University of Ghana or Ibadan acquired in five years.

The skills contained in the curriculum represent the great forces at the command of modern society. Introduced into tribal or traditional or underdeveloped countries, they have the power to construct or disrupt, to advance or to confuse. As some sort of guideline to the ensuing discussion it is clearly the lesson of the past ten years that the use of these forces calls for "planfulness," for coordination, for interdisciplinary analysis, in short, for a flexible, watchful, and constructive strategy. Strategy is used in several senses. Principally, it is the strategy of progressive change, or the strategy of emergent adjustment. All meanings lay the greatest stress on flexibility and adjustment. In education they rank above dogma, doctrine and tradition.

The establishment of universities, especially in Africa, was an accompaniment of the various political settlements. The first academic charters and statutes had some of the optimistic and dogmatic character of the political constitutions. They revealed the same confidence in the university as the constitutions revealed in parliamentary government. Both depended upon a tried and settled body of institutional arrangements, of conventional techniques, of traditional subjects of concern, and upon an accepted standard of behavior and achievement. Both were mature and tested instruments capable of bearing the responsibilities assigned to them in their own national environment.

The new African universities of British form were founded in a spirit that was admirable. The conviction was admirable that excellence in building, staffing, and curriculum was a rich and honorable legacy to be left by former rulers. This conviction was carried out with integrity and generosity. There was the deepest pride in the university as an uncorrupt environment, governed by an elect, ministering only to the best minds, protected against the immediate noise of marketplace and factory, shielded from the importunities of government. A number of the newer universities came into being just before the fresh breeze of new thought about the role of the university began to sweep away the traditionalism, the entrenched privileges, and the doctrinaire quality of much British university thinking. Instead of the most modern university, the British academic world had as by accident exported an anachronism. The definition of excellence was carried within a formula that lacked flexibility. From the beginning the new African universities were invested with attitudes that made them appear far more detached from their environment than the older institutions after which they were modeled, although it is a curious delusion of the British that their universities are singularly pure in their independence of government and their freedom from governmental influence. At the outset there were bred misunderstandings, misinterpretations, and political resentments that made later adjustments more difficult. There was lost the invaluable early advantage of defining the role of the university as one bringing it immediately and concretely close to the task of building a new nation. There was insufficient awareness of the inescapably close interdependence of government and university in a new country, of the wholeness of all education, of the need for the trained university mind to apply itself to the urgent problems of the day. University autonomy and academic freedom were given doctrinaire connotations that sounded strange and excessive, even in metropolitan ears. Those functions that belonged together in a new country grew up separately, responsibilities that could be most beneficially shared were divided, and communication became difficult. One saw the phenomenon of an institution devoted to tradition, beside a government that could only succeed by breaking with tradition.

Sir Eric Ashby has given the most measured account with illustrations of the difficult problem of university adaptation and adjustment in a new environment in his book, *Universities: British,*

Indian, African. Both wisely and generously he uses his comments to the constructive end of describing and stressing the spirit of adjustment that began to replace the first doctrinaire formalism. That all universities everywhere are timeless institutions is explained by their powers of regeneration.

Sir Eric Ashby pays a tribute to the idea of relevance introduced into African education from America. This is the American spirit of helpful attentiveness to the major needs of the national environment. It would however, be smug and self-centered not to recognize that analogies, doctrines, and dogmas are just as much pitfalls for the American academic mind when working on the task of educational development in new countries. Otherwise, there would not be the need to put so much emphasis on innovation, adaptation, and strategy.

There is little wisdom in a listing of error and inadequacy unless it serves as a guide to more discerning future action. The lesson of the past score years overwhelmingly emphasizes relevance, adaptation, adjustment, flexibility, freedom from dogma. Harbison advocates a "strategy of human resource development." This is a technique of studying and responding to emergent phenomena. It is a discerning and conscientious pragmatism of the trained mind that seeks new methods of analysis, fresh insights, and guidance to action drawn from the facts as they exist in a country at emerging stages of its development.

A strategy of development is not a superior form of generalship exercised from some metropolis, or administered by a panel of experts. It is rather a continuing watchfulness, an awareness of function, of relationship, a disposition to flexible adjustment, a tempering of compulsive wishfulness by economic and social realities. It is therefore a responsibility widely shared. In education a proper sense of strategy has at least two principal requirements. The first is an insistence on seeing the wholeness of education above its conventional sectors and institutions. The second is the recognition of education as a primary and not as an auxiliary factor in national development. These requirements enjoin an abandonment of the assumption that there exists a benign free market economy in education and its products. Ignorance, illiteracy, a deficiency of skills are all marks of underdevelopment. A great and urgent need for education does not confer an immediate absorptive capacity for all and any education in an underdeveloped society. The knowledge that unplanned educational development can have disruptive effects is a difficult lesson to accept.

Economic dislocation, social breakdown, the inequities of a free market economy are familiar indictments against the regime of colonialism. As phenomena under a regime of self-government they have not ceased. One could argue that the road to development and modernization must perforce pass through dislocation, instability, severe political and social instability. If, however, we accept the historical judgment that the vast area of vacuum, void, and insufficiency constitutes one of the two major crises of the modern world, complacent arguments are too dangerous to accept.

Examples of dislocation and imbalance presumably caused by education are not warnings against education itself. Instead they are inducements to using and adapting education to avoid and minimize these consequences in the interests of more profitable and constructive development. The classic example of dislocation and imbalance, familiar throughout much of Africa, comes from primary education. In Accra, Lagos, Ibadan, Kampala, Nairobi, great populations have moved in from the countryside. They are encampments on the frontier of the modern world, encampments of men hoping to use their scanty knowledge to lead a better life. Still patiently they await the prosperity, the employment, and the standard of living to which they feel that they have gained a title. If education, even of the incompletest sort, causes large populations to abandon a sector of agricultural production, which needs them, in order to flock to an urban sector which clearly does not, then a beneficial agency has created disruptive and possibly explosive forces. One of the most disturbing developments in Africa is precisely the drainage of people from agriculture, which economic analysis shows to be the most important sector, into the ghettos of the towns. It is an unprofitable exchange of rural subsistence for urban poverty, of employment for unemployment, of tolerable rural discontent for a dangerous urban frustration.

Two further areas of education are illustrative. They are postsecondary education and secondary education itself. The dramatic growth of university education was not accompanied by a compensating growth in the education of supportive personnel. In America phrases such as the "umbrella concept" of university education, of the "inclined plane" or the "escalator" describe a balanced production of highly skilled leadership together with the essential auxiliary support without which government officials, business managers, and professional men lose their full effectiveness. A university system that is mainly concerned with the education of men for elite positions may cause the neglect of an area of higher education which provides the supportive skills on which its graduates must depend. Thus, unwittingly, the university that maintains itself on a single plateau of academic performance introduces a damaging distortion in professional and economic activity.

In Africa the position of the university as the only attractive form of higher education tends to imbalance and warp the system of secondary education. A healthy system of secondary education sends its students onward along three thoroughfares or axes. The first leads directly to employment. The second leads to further training for the essential second-level supportive careers. The third leads to specialized and mostly university education. Where the university axis is favored and patronized at the expense of the other, then what Benjamin Disraeli called the "two worlds" tend to be repeated in African society. One is the world of literate, well-salaried elite of government officials and professional men. Their habits, needs and consumption are those of an industrial society. Their dependence on marketable exports and industrial imports brings them closer to the metropolitan outside world than to much of their own population. The few may therefore promote institutions and arrangements that actually make more difficult the promotion of the needs of the many. An attendant phenomenon of serious consequences to the universities is the gradual crowding of the graduates into the still narrow, limited, and superficially thin areas of modern salaried employment. Frustration in the small world of opportunity and reward, and frustration in the great world of little opportunity and limited reward are twin threats to stability.

It is obviously no longer possible to take the view, common in advanced societies, that each step taken by science, technology, and education is a positive and favorable addition to the accumulating sum of benefit and progress that takes a young society from backwardness to enlightenment, increases its prosperity, and enhances its stability. Since forces, good in themselves, can be the cause of disharmony, it becomes necessary to develop new methods of appraisal and action. The essential point to emphasize is that education, including university education, is functionally related to the economic and productive structure of its own society.

In the developing countries the need is clearly for a studied and planned partnership of education with other factors of development. This lesson is hard to learn, and difficult to argue, because it seems to conflict with passionately held convictions on the rights of men to be relieved of ignorance. One needs only spend a short time with an eloquent spokesman like Mr. Mboya to feel his entire conviction that no limits must be put on the training and output of university graduates, or therefore on the expansion of universities. The conventional academic mind is inclined to resist what looks like a mercantile linkage of the requirements of the mind with productivity, profit, the labor force, and investment. Assertion of this linkage can still arouse suspicion and heat over intellectual and academic freedom. In an advanced society the linkage exists, but with less conscious involvement of the intellectual in the planning and management of the national development. In developing countries the linkage must be more saliently identified and cultivated. Education cannot acceptably withdraw its attention and concern from the most important economic requirements of a young society. The most advantageous productive sectors must be served by a supply of trained manpower. Investment in education must show favor to areas and levels of education that are in economic demand. A selection of priorities and a planned allocation of resources cannot be avoided.

The proper role of American universities and American assistance is to sustain and encourage national plans or strategies of development. To that end it becomes especially important that we have both in government and in the universities a special category of university trained experts. They should obviously be experts who can feel, think and advise from *within* the countries or areas with which they deal. They should have minds schooled to think about education without compartments, from elementary education upwards to graduate training. Their thought must be receptive to the knowledge that comes from economics, demography, statistics, political science, and sociology. Above all their minds must be capable of discerning or accepting new patterns in education in order to find answers to the developmental needs of a new country.

It should be emphasized again that there can be no thought of placing developing countries under the academic tutelage of foreign experts. But greater insurance is needed that assistance programs and American university activities have the benefit of a means of review that is current. Adjustment and adaptation as a continuous process are a central secret of cooperation in national strategies of development.

When one comes to the question of the machinery and methods of cooperation between universities and government, there is wisdom in a cautious and exploratory approach. He would be an undiscerning man who claimed that we have a successful and efficient means of communication between higher education and government. He would also be a rash man who claimed to possess a formula for the most profitable relationship between the two sectors. There is no logic of French administrative discipline and clarity that could be introduced to govern this relationship. Instead of the clubbiness of discourse which British universities use among themselves and with government, the American university system has dozens or scores of associations, none of them cen-

39

tral or fully representative. The prestigious name, Association of American Universities, is mostly sound. It gives no leadership at all. This phenomenon expresses the free wheeling pluralism of the university world. The free jostling of the academic marketplace is supposed to produce a healthy and creative diversity. The more eminent the university the more piously its president talks of the blessedness of laissez-faire, as he moves down the dredged channels to the sources of university support. Every educator knows the supporting arguments and has used them. Educators are even slower than businessmen in admitting the role of government in financing and shaping the university.

In the widening areas of government and university activity in international relations, an organic, reliable, experienced, interested, continuous, and available means of communication must now be developed. These six words are deliberately set down. Of them the greatest are *experience, continuity,* and *reliability.* These words and remarks are intended to apply most specially to the area of government and university effort in educational and developmental assistance abroad. To think and act in terms of a continuous, unfolding strategy calls for considerable experience and trained judgment.

The greater importance of education in international affairs does and will attract men of high ability into government service. Yet in the area of education it seems urgent to speak against the hazards of too extreme an internal professionalization of governmental educational policy, and equally urgent to speak for an adequate mechanism of reliable and continuous consultation with the best experience in the universities.

The Agency for International Development has had very extensive responsibility for education programs. It has had valuable successes. It has had poor and wasteful failures. It cannot be said that the Agency is throughout marked by a jealous bureaucratic compartmentalism. There has been a very remarkable willingness to seek and to use the advice of educational leaders. The major and damaging weakness in the Agency's relations with universities and education is not a neglect of communication. But it has been an inability to prevent communication and consultation from being confused and fragmented by the many voices with which education speaks. In the files of the Agency there are probably more reports by committees and teams than anywhere else in government. Distinguished names appear once or twice rarely to return again. Intermittence and discontinuity can hardly lead to structural planning.

The need for various consultative bodies exists. One discerns this with disturbing clarity in the underdeveloped countries themselves. If it is agreed that answers must be found, they will be best if they are based upon the men, the qualities and the conditions described by the six words—organic, reliable, experienced, interested, continuous, and available.

In this effort to draw salient outlines on a very broad canvas there are bound to be omissions. Were this a book or a series of lectures it would be logical to enter upon a full discussion of the actual experience of cooperation between universities and government in the field of foreign assistance during the past fifteen years. In a presentation which places so much emphasis upon forward planning and a strategy for future action, a brief, suggestive glance at some elements of strategy should provoke discussion.

A decision to develop a progressive, adaptive approach to educational assistance in developing countries seems to be the only way for governmental agencies like AID to extricate themselves from some of the less rewarding habits and practices of the past fifteen years. Friends and foes of assistance programs join in wishing for a new appraisal of future action. The President himself requested Ambassador Edward M. Korry to undertake such an appraisal. Ambassador Korry's report is likely to be viewed with respect and suspicion. The respect is for the President's interest and the high competence of his chosen agent, Ambassador Korry. Suspicion is aroused by the fear that the report, as it passes through the channels and arteries of a complex agency, will be moved slowly back into the files. These are not intended to be irreverent words. They are intended to stress once more that the sort of "planfulness" which the President properly seeks cannot be set down in a single document. It has to be elaborated by a continuing process. This process must be deliberate and properly organized.

We have seen how difficult it was for universities to depart from their own traditions and habits. The public sector of government has the same difficulty. Procedures that were devised years ago in order to draw upon the resources of universities have not always risen above the first levels of improvisation. There is no way of avoiding the question whether university resources are being put to their best use in developing countries. Any careful review of university contracts makes it clear that they are not uniform. They range from the very good to the very bad. Some are responsibly and conscientiously carried out. There are notoriously a number of contracts that present an unlovely picture of casualness and neglect. The standing of a university at home is not always a guarantee of its performance abroad. At home university contracts are sometimes worn like badges, a conversation piece at fund raising dinners. In the field some of them are academic orphans.

The history of university contracts points to a number of important lessons. Those contracts are most beneficial where the university is so interested that it will devote members of its own permanent administrative and teaching staff to their service. Those contracts are less beneficial where a team is hired in the academic marketplace and imperfectly and remotely supervised from the home university. Instances have occurred where most of the members of an overseas contract team had seen the home university for the first time when they were hired, and did not expect to see it after the contract had expired. One must express real doubt whether the present contract system adequately succeeds in five important respects. They are put forward as possible tests for an improved use of our academic resources in a more deeply cooperative strategy with developing countries.

Present contracts do not tap all available resources in the total system of American higher education. Manpower recruitment for contracts compares unfavorably with British and French methods of recruitment in obtaining the services of men at the higher levels of academic experience and accomplishment. The position of the contract activity in the structure and the academic arrangements of the overseas institution varies from healthy partnership to an uneasy separateness. The experiences gained through the contract activity do not flow sufficiently back into the contracting university as an enrichment and ferment in its own curriculum and academic life. The final weakness of the contract system might more wisely be stated as a question. What valuable legacy of permanent intellectual and institutional bonds, exchanges, and even interdependence is thoughtfully being prepared to succeed the formal contract period? The answer is not clear.

These comments go to the heart of the problems shared by the universities and government. They are not intended to set off another outbreak of the rumbling uneasiness felt by both sides, although it may be well to be reminded of the very real embarrassments and handicaps which exist on both sides. The bonds of cooperation between government and university in the greatest variety of international activities are essential and irreplaceable. Any criticism or discussion must be aimed at their enrichment, their improvement, their reinforcement.

President Johnson's recommendations on support to the universities in international education would acquire their greatest value if the strength they gave at home showed itself in greater effectiveness abroad. It would be a tragedy if domestic and international interests in this field were departmentally and functionally unplanned and uncoordinated. The strengthening of the curriculum, the heightened attractiveness to students of international studies and careers, and most especially the increase in staff positions can and should be so designed as to improve performance in the five respects mentioned above. Let it be emphasized beyond any doubt that in each of these respects the deepest benefit of the developing countries has equal status with the deepest benefit of the American university system. The Camelot incident made public what experienced men knew already. The national interest in research is great. The crisis of American consciousness of the modern world demands it. But the high national interest in helping the developing world out of its emptiness into the fullness of modern development would not be served if a tidal wave of graduate students and professors washed overseas, with too little concern for the urgent need for help in men and their skills.

A final historic note will drive this point home. There have been developing countries before. These also needed to import skills. In the nineteenth century Australia, for example, gave permanent residence and citizenship in exchange for skills. No one has ever succeeded in assessing the balance of exchanges. In the twentieth century most developing countries will not barter permanent residence and citizenship for imports of skill and talent. This attitude is part of the substance of their nationalism. Yet without skills they cannot develop. They have available three answers.

In schools and universities they can produce their own skills. They can export untrained minds and reimport them after training overseas. But in any reckoning there is an unfilled measure of need for which the import of alien or expatriate skills seems to be the best answer. It must be, in the political interest of the new countries, a temporary answer. That is conceded. It is far from clear, however, that there is any sensible balance between these three answers. Certainly all concerned in the United States have not established as good an answer to the supply of expatriate personnel as the need demands. Yet for the United States the obligation has peculiar force. No nation, not even ancient Rome, has benefited so much from the import of skills. The phenomenon of the brain drain even today surely imposes on this country an obligation to redress this great imbalance by some well-planned measure. The export of American skill is the greatest contribution the university can make.

Development and Utilization
of Human Resources:

Building a System for Assistance Activities

Frederick
Harbison

The argument presented in this paper rests upon two assumptions. The first is that one objective of U.S. foreign policy is to help accelerate economic and social development of the less developed parts of the world. There should be no argument about this as a stated goal of foreign policy, although there is, of course, a major question about the amount of resources the American people may be willing to devote to it. Accordingly, it would be more realistic to rephrase this goal as follows: The policy of the United States is to devote limited financial and human resources to assisting the less developed countries, and to use these limited resources in such a way as to make the maximum contribution to the economic and social development of the assisted countries.

The second assumption, which may be open to debate, is that the most important determinant of progress in the less developed countries will be their capacity to develop and to effectively utilize (or employ) their human resources. Capital and natural resources are passive agents. The prime movers of modernization are human beings who accumulate capital, exploit natural resources, and build organizations to provide goods and services in the broadest sense. If a country is unable to develop the skills and brains of its people and to involve them usefully in the progressive building of a society, then it cannot develop much else. In the end, the wealth and viability of modern nations depends upon their human resources.

With these two assumptions, we may derive a principle of foreign policy: The United States can best help the less developed countries by concentrating the major portion of its resources available for assistance on strategic measures to enable these countries effectively to develop and utilize their human resources.

Admittedly, the United States is neither inclined nor able to provide all the assistance which the less developed countries will demand or need, and for this reason it should exercise reserve and modesty in its proclamations about what it can and will do to help. But, at the same time, it is to the advantage of both the United States and these countries to utilize assistance resources as productively and efficiently as possible. The purpose of this paper is to suggest some modest steps which might be taken to help achieve this objective.

In looking back over the past two decades, we should neither exaggerate the accomplishments nor minimize the shortcomings of our efforts. For example, U.S. economists, along with their colleagues in other countries, have dramatized the notion that expenditures for education are investments which can win high economic returns. This idea has taken root in developing countries. In most, the proportion of national income being devoted to education is rising rapidly. Yet, in many, there is obvious over-investment in the wrong kinds of education. In some cases, education can and does retard rather than promote economic and social progress. The overemphasis on purely quantitative cost-benefit analysis of expenditures for education may obscure proper considerations of quality, orientation, balance, and noneconomic goals. The real problem in the developing countries today is not that they are investing too little in education, but rather that they are often wasting scarce resources in building an educational system which is inadequately geared to their needs for social and economic development. It is now clear that political and social pressures are forcing the developing countries to commit ever-increasing proportions of their resources to education, so that the crucial problem is to find ways for them to get a greater social and economic benefit for their expenditure.

Manpower surveys as a basis for educational planning have been marketed vigorously in the underdeveloped countries. On the whole they have provided useful benchmarks for human resource development. Yet, as in the case of cost-benefit analysis of investments in education, they have stressed quantitative over qualitative criteria. And, for the most part, they have dealt exclusively with high-level manpower requirements for the modern sector. Almost without exception, they have avoided consideration of problems of mounting unemployment in urban areas and chronic underemployment in the traditional sectors. Yet, in countries with high rates of population growth, these problems are probably more critical and certainly more difficult to solve than those associated with the education and training of high-level manpower.

U.S. aid to the developing countries has stressed higher education, and it has emphasized the central importance of teacher training for effective expansion of formal education systems. This emphasis is on the whole sound. But, relatively little attention

45

has been given to the relevancy of what is being taught to the local environment. And very little consideration has been given to improvement of training provided by employing institutions which, after all, play just as important a role as formal education in the process of human resource development.

The university-to-university contract relationship was an important American innovation of the last decade, and in the future it will continue to be an effective means of assistance. But, here there have been shortcomings too. In some cases, the American staffs provided have been of questionable competence, and their commitment to long-range service has been too limited. Some projects, moreover, have been directed to low-priority needs. And, in too many cases, there is only a minimal understanding of the logic of individual projects in a broad strategy of assistance and quite ineffective liaison with other related projects in the country or area.

To be sure, we have made significant forward strides in bringing persons from the less developed countries to the United States for education and training. Some of the benefits are clear. But, there are instances where overemphasis on education in the U.S. has impeded the most constructive development of local institutions in the assisted countries. And overexposure to life in the advanced countries may have contributed, at least in part, to a brain drain from such countries.

In the future the urgent problems faced by the developing countries may be quite different from those which commanded the greatest attention in the last decade. For example, many of the developing countries have been preoccupied with the problems of industrialization and the consequent urgency of producing more scientists, engineers and technologists in the universities. This concern will continue, but there is growing awareness that the technical and human problems of industrialization are much easier to solve than the more intractable problems of agricultural production and rural development. The significant failures in meeting development targets have been in the agricultural rather than the modern manufacturing and commercial sectors. Some economists, indeed, are now saying that the highest priority problem in many countries will not be the increase in national income but rather the avoidance of outright starvation. Thus, in the decades ahead there is likely to be a more urgent concern with the financial, organizational, and human resources required to achieve a rural transformation as a basis for an eventual industrial revolution.

In the past, there has been an implicit assumption that, with proper assistance, the less developed parts of the world could catch up with advanced countries. There is cause to believe today, however, that despite substantial progress in many newly developing countries, the gap between the rich and poor nations is likely to widen rather than narrow. Even more sobering are the growing disparities between the modern and traditional sectors within the developing countries themselves.

In the past, the developing countries have been rightly concerned with production of high-level manpower to meet clearly identifiable shortages. Yet as progress is made on this front, it is becoming apparent that the developing countries are often unable to retain and effectively utilize the precious talent which they are producing at such tremendous cost. The current worry over the brain drain and the so-called technological gap is a case in point.

In the last decade, the high rate of population growth in the developing countries was giving planners cause for concern. But in the future, the population problem is likely to reach crisis proportions. Rising birth rates are likely to postpone for decades the achievement of universal primary education, the attainment of full employment opportunities, and even decent standards of health and nutrition. Thus, in the future, strategies of human resource development and utilization will have to include concerted efforts toward birth limitation.

Finally, as the euphoria of independence and the period of "the golden handshake" recede into the past, many of the newly developing countries are becoming grimly aware of the fact that the path of economic growth is strewn with obstacles and hard choices, that external human and financial resources for expensive new universities and technical institutes are limited, and that desirable and seemingly necessary programs for educational expansion may have to be foregone in order to give highest priority to those which are absolutely indispensable. In the near future, the needs for human resource development, as seen by both the developing countries and those attempting to assist them, will certainly exceed the capabilities for meeting them. Aspirations are already running ahead of reasonable possibilities of achievement, and the resulting frustration may well result in widespread rising resentment.

The honeymoon stage is over. Neither we nor the developing countries can afford to devote energy and resources to *all* projects which appear to be useful, desirable, or generally helpful in providing understanding and communication between nations. The granting of assistance for projects which are most readily acceptable to the host country rather than for those having the greatest multiplier effect is a luxury we can no longer afford. The initiation of pilot programs which are too ambitious and too costly ever to be supported by local resources needs examination. It makes no sense to transfer American standards, ideas, and institutions to developing countries unless they can be adapted to local environments. An *ad hoc* piece-by-piece approach to assistance, no matter how well-rationalized in humanitarian terms or justified on experimental grounds, will no longer suffice. It is time to develop, with the collaboration of the host countries, a mentality of assistance which will stress the integrated analysis of problems of development and utilization of human resources as well as the notion of strategy building based upon the examination of alternatives and the choice of priorities. The remainder of this paper is devoted to the means of developing such a mentality.

ANALYSIS OF SYSTEMS OF HUMAN RESOURCE DEVELOPMENT AND UTILIZATION

In order to solve problems one must understand them. And it might be useful to think of the processes of human resource development and utilization as constituting a system—a system which in some respects may be analogous to a system for generation, distribution, and use of electric power. (I must confess that this thought was generated in my mind by the gigantic New York power failure in the fall of 1965!) One can identify skill generating centers, such as schools, universities, training institutes, and employing organizations which develop people on the job. The linkages between such centers are analogous to transmission lines. The manpower problems encountered by developing countries such as skill shortages and labor surpluses may be thought of as attributable to power failures in particular generating centers, ineffective linkages between these centers, or faulty design resulting in the failure of the total system to carry the loads expected of it. A system of human skill generation, like a system of electric power generation, should be designed to carry varying loads; it must have built-in flexibility to meet such loads; it must be adequate in size; and above all its components should be properly balanced. A "systems analysis approach" makes it easier to identify in operational terms major problem areas, and it compels the analyst to examine the critical interrelationships between various manpower, education, and national development programs. It provides a logical starting point for building a strategy of human resource development.

From a policy standpoint, the underlying purpose in examining a system is to discover ways of making it work better. One cannot expect at the outset to have a very definitive or sophisticated understanding of the operation of the system, but it is possible to identify, at least tentatively, certain critical points where some judicious tinkering could yield good results. This is the essence of strategy-building. If we expect our efforts to have a multiplier effect on a country's development and utilization of human resources, some analysis of this kind is essential.

In the typical less-developed country, the general system of human resource development and utilization may be understood best by an integrated analysis of five component systems. For convenience let us label these component systems as follows: (1) employment generation, (2) formal education, (3) training and development in employment, (4) movements of manpower with critical skills, and (5) planning and strategy development. Examination of the first four systems provides an understanding of the dynamics of human resource development and utilization; the fifth gives an indication of what a country may be doing to improve the operation of the system as a whole.

Employment generation. As economies develop, they create opportunities for people to engage in productive activities (in providing both goods and a variety of services) which hopefully increase their real wealth and that of the nation. This process, however, seldom works perfectly. Depending on the course which development follows, there are shortages of persons with critical skills or knowledge and surpluses of people seeking opportunities which the economy cannot provide. Shortages and surpluses of manpower are to some extent related, the former often being a partial explanation for the latter.

In contrast with the advanced countries, the employment generation systems in the less-developed world are very distorted. Both skill shortages and manpower surpluses are much more pronounced. The disparities between the so-called modern and traditional sectors are wide. High wages, modern technology, improved managerial practices, and high productivity strictly limit the capacity of the modern sector to absorb labor, whereas high rates of population growth, rising aspirations, and exposure to education swell the ranks of those seeking entry into this sector. The traditional sector cannot provide an adequate market for the products of the modern, and it often fails to supply sufficient food for the masses of underemployed and unemployed urban dwellers. In many developing countries, therefore, open unemployment is associated with unbalanced modernization. Unemployment appears to be a by-product of growth, a disease of industrialization, and a consequence of introduction of modern ideas and institutions. Its

49

roots lie not in failure to achieve high levels of investment and economic growth, but paradoxically in progress toward achievement of these very goals. This is at least a partial explanation of the ever-growing masses of unemployed school leavers.

Some of the more critical points to examine in the employment generation system are the following: The structure of skills required for rural and agricultural development as well as expansion of the modern sector; the present and projected capacity of the modern sector to absorb manpower; a comparison of this with present and projected outputs of the formal education system; a comparison of earning possibilities of those engaged in the modern sector and those in the traditional sectors; and an analysis of the operation of the wage and salary structure in the modern sector in inducing persons to prepare for and enter the more productive activities. In comparison with the situation a few years ago, considerable thought is being given now to this range of problems, and techniques of analysis and preliminary findings are becoming available.*

Formal education. In many respects, the system of formal education in a developing country is the easiest to understand. The educational pyramid can be analyzed; teacher requirements may be calculated and projected; drop-out and wastage rates can be identified; and the orientation and objectives of education, particularly at the higher levels, may be determined. Since in less developed economies educational systems are generally underdeveloped, the pressure of expansion at almost any level is commonly recognized. Thus, the difficult task is to establish priority of needs within the constraints of limited resources. The problem is to chart a course of growth in the educational system which is in balance with and related to a country's planned course of economic, social, and political development. And this means that the system of education must be examined in relationship to the system of employment generation.

Among the more critical points for analysis are these: (a) *access* to educational opportunity, (b) *orientation*, or the concept of the function of education, (c) *outputs* of the education industry, (d) *resource constraints*, both human and financial, which limit the rate of expansion of educational programs, and (e) *flexibility* to meet changing economic and social needs.

---

* See for example, W. Arthur Lewis, *Development Planning*, Harper and Row, New York, 1966, particularly Chapter 5 entitled "Unemployment." Also for more detailed analysis of employment generation, there is a paper by the author, "The Generation of Employment in Newly Developing Countries" (available in preliminary mimeographed form at the Industrial Relations Section, Princeton University, Princeton, New Jersey).

In developing societies the opportunities for education are limited, and thus it is important to determine who has *access* to them and why. Among the possible factors determining access are geographical location, income of parents, tribal or political affiliation, intellectual capacity, quality of education at lower levels (as a determinant of access to higher levels of education), and availability of scholarships. It is important to examine access to each level of the educational system (primary, secondary, higher, and other) as well as to examine each type (technical, academic, vocational, teacher training and various university faculties).

The *orientation* of the educational system is critically important. Is the system oriented largely to preparation for ultimate entry into higher education? Is it designed to educate the masses or to generate an elite? Is the aim of vocational schools to develop specific skills or to provide reasonably broad pre-employment education? Are the methods and content of education at various levels realistically related to the local environment? And what is the relative emphasis on science and engineering as compared with arts, humanities and the law in university education?

The *outputs* of the education system at various points are also significant. How many pupils who enter the first grade complete the primary school cycle? What are their chances of entering the secondary? How many students having access to secondary schools eventually graduate, and of these what proportion enter and complete courses of higher education? These are logical quantitative measures of output, but where possible, they should be expressed in qualitative dimensions as well. In most countries, it is relatively easy to check the outputs of the education system and to relate them to requirements or absorbtive capacity as determined by the employment generation system.

A more difficult task is the analysis of *resource constraints*. In nearly all countries, the costs of education are rising as a proportion both of government expenditure and national income. What are the existing and possible revenue sources to meet rising costs at the local, regional, and national levels? The human resource restraints, moreover, are even more significant. How does the system produce and set aside "seed-corn" resources in the form of teaching personnel? What quantities of teachers are required? How can persons qualified to teach be diverted from alternative occupations? And at what economic and social cost?

Another check is for *flexibility*. Progressive change is the very essence of modernization, and thus it is difficult to predict the precise occupational structure of any economy for any stage of development. To what extent, therefore, does the educational system produce people who are versatile and adaptable? How sensitive is the system to unexpected changes in social and economic needs? Or more specifically, are vocational schools training persons narrowly for crafts for which demand may be uncertain instead of providing basic education which may be applicable for a variety of occupations? A system of generation of skills and knowledge must be capable of carrying unexpected loads, meeting emergencies which were not anticipated, and casting off burdens which prove to be no longer necessary.

In any analysis of an educational system, the role of higher education should be singled out for particular attention. The university "subsystem" casts its shadow over the educational system as a whole. It tends to mold the curriculum at the primary and secondary levels; it is the high-prestige segment of the education system; and it is one of the strategic gateways for entry into a country's elite. Universities and other institutions of higher learning are also important centers for research on social and economic problems; they are producers as well as disseminators of knowledge. The university subsystem, therefore, plays a strategic role in the gearing of the education system to the country's basic needs, and in this respect it may facilitate the achievement of proper balance or produce far-reaching distortions in the entire system of human resource development and utilization.

Training and development in employment. In most countries, relatively few persons receive specific training in schools prior to employment; most are trained in the course of employment. Ideally, a good system of formal education produces broadly trainable rather than specifically trained people. The training function, as such, is largely a responsibility of employing institutions as well as the life-time concern of the individual himself. In analyzing human resource development, therefore, it is important to look at training-in-employment as a distinct system, separate from but hopefully closely related to the education system.

In developing countries, the most obvious manpower trainers are the public services and the medium and large sized private enterprises. Normally, they have both informal and formal programs for selection, training and upgrading employees. In the smaller enterprises and family establishments, there is usually an indigenous apprenticeship system. In rural areas, farmers are trained mostly by their fathers, with assistance perhaps from agricultural extension workers. Through a myriad of activities of this kind, men gain experience, and this is a major dimension of human resource development.

Some of the more critical questions for study are these: What

2

are the principal patterns and processes of training-in-employment, and what are their outstanding strengths and weaknesses? What are the main points of contact between the educational system and the training system? What training activities are provided in schools which could be provided as effectively by employing institutions? What forces induce employing institutions to provide training, and what incentives are appropriate to encourage them to shoulder more responsibility in this area? For the most part, manpower and education planners, being preoccupied with analysis of formal education systems, have tended to neglect this range of questions, and as a result, they have overloaded many education systems with training burdens they simply cannot bear.

The movement of manpower with critical skills. Because of skill shortages, developing countries must often import high-level manpower from abroad. This may take place through technical assistance, establishment of foreign enterprises, hiring of contract personnel, or immigration. At the same time, these countries lose some of their best educated and critically needed manpower to advanced countries—a process often referred to as "the brain drain." It is important, therefore, to determine both the inward and outward flows of high-level manpower, and to ascertain the forces which account for this movement. The internal movement within a country, moreover, is just as significant as the external. The spread of education, and the growing disparities between the modern and traditional sectors usually cause a brain drain also from the rural to the urban areas. And characteristically, the deployment of highly educated and trained persons for work in the rural areas encounters great resistance. The system of human resource development and utilization therefore can suffer great power losses through both internal and external losses of talent.

The external brain drain is attributable only in part to higher wages and other attractions in the advanced countries. High-level manpower is also forced out of the developing countries sometimes as a result of political situations but more often as a consequence of basic weaknesses in a country's education and employment generation systems. For example, the machinery for matching skills and jobs is usually underdeveloped. Scientists pour out of universities at home and abroad before research organizations in the developing countries are created to make productive use of their services. This in a sense is analogous to investing in jet airplanes before plans are completed to build the airport runways to accommodate them.

The mounting concern over the flow of skilled manpower highlights the importance of analysis of the system of external and internal movements of high-level manpower. The argument here is that this problem should be studied not as an isolated and unique phenomenon but rather as a part of a broader complex of related problems in a country's general system of development and utilization of human resources.

Planning and strategy development. The ultimate objective of analyzing the systems of employment generation, formal education, training-in-employment, and movements of skilled manpower is to identify some of the major weaknesses and inconsistencies in human resource development and utilization and to formulate appropriate remedial measures. This is the essence of planning and strategy development. The crucial questions, then, are these: What consideration has been given by development planners to human resource problems? Have they recognized the need for integrated analysis of the systems discussed above? What machinery, if any, has been set up to study any one or all of these systems? And to what extent have plans been implemented after their formulation? The answers to these questions are usually discouraging. In most countries, very little has been accomplished, and here may be an area where assistance from the outside might have its greatest multiplier effect.

The analysis of systems which has been proposed can be undertaken globally or intensively. In most cases, it must be initiated modestly. Statistics, hard facts, and reliable information are difficult to find. Initial tentative conclusions must stem from judgments, informal opinions, and intuition. Yet, it is just as important to have at least a sketchy concept of the operation of a system as a whole as it is to amass detailed information about a few of its components. As the sources of information improve and as better techniques of analysis become available, the understanding of the system may become progressively more sophisticated. The distinction between "horseback judgments" and computerized analysis based upon formal models is only a matter of degree. The study of human resource systems can and must progress from simple to more complex kinds of analysis within the constraints of available information. In this paper, we have simply suggested an *approach* toward understanding of human resource problems rather than a blueprint for specific analysis. Essentially, this approach rests on the trite but true premise that the finding of definitive empirical answers is dependent upon asking the right questions.

SOME PRACTICAL PROPOSALS

Is it possible to build the competence and machinery for integrated analysis of systems of human resource development and utilization in other countries as a basis for foreign policy? The answer, I think, is yes. Presumably, we attempt integrated analysis in other areas of foreign policy. Why not in this one also? The following measures might be worthy of consideration.

First, efforts could be made to encourage our representatives abroad to take a more analytical and strategy-building approach to human resource problems in the developing countries. For example, there are in the embassies and the Agency for International Development missions quite a number of persons involved in education, manpower, and cultural affairs. They could be instructed to develop for each country a framework for the integrated analysis of problems of human resource development and utilization, and required to justify specific projects and proposals in terms of it. As suggested above, the initial analysis may have to be rather sketchy. At the outset, the important objective would be primarily to develop the approach or mentality of integrated analysis and strategy building. It should be possible to arrange short training courses in Washington, informal seminars in the various countries, and occasional regional conferences in the field as a means of building interest and participation in developing this approach. It would be appropriate, moreover, to have the participation of foundation representatives and other aid-giving organizations in programs of this kind.

Second, it would be desirable to establish a supportive organization to provide information and assistance to the U.S. Government representatives abroad. This organization could employ a corps of human resource specialists who would be available, upon request, to assist these representatives in constructing their analytical frameworks as well as in planning and conducting seminars and training programs. As part of its mission, the "back-stopping" organization would be responsible for keeping abreast of the current activities following closely the progress made in each country, and informing the representatives in each country about what is being done in the others. It would not be necessary for this organization to be part of a particular government agency. Indeed, it might be more appropriately a private institution operating under a government contract and perhaps supported in part by foundation grants. The central function of this organization would be to provide technical assistance for U.S. field personnel. It would not be responsible for policy formulation, and it would not itself conduct basic research.

Third, under the new International Education Act, funds could be provided to support a range of research projects in American universities and colleges. A broader knowledge about the processes of human resource development and utilization would be in itself important for understanding the culture, the aspirations, and the social and economic problems of foreign countries. At the same time, research in the field could lead to development of new approaches, improved techniques of analysis, and substantive findings based upon global experience. Thus, the research program would provide both the theoretical and empirical foundations for greater understanding of other societies as well as for integrated analysis and strategy building for assistance to developing nations.

Finally, the American educational community now has an opportunity, if not indeed a responsibility, to participate in the formulation of U.S. foreign policy in this very vital area of strategy building. In the past, American universities have been asked to undertake specific assignments in foreign countries. Seldom have they understood fully the relationship of their particular projects to a broader plan of assistance. On the contrary they have assumed quite naïvely that someone in high office somewhere had a logical strategy in mind. But, only in rare cases has this been a valid assumption.

U.S. institutions of higher learning have the competence (and are in a position to get the resources) to assist and, in some cases, to lead a movement for more systematic analysis and strategy building in this area of foreign policy. They should not always hide under the umbrella of research, leaving it to others to judge its usefulness or relevance to the issues of the day. And if universities are to continue to operate technical assistance projects in developing countries, they ought to contribute also to evolving the overall grand design for making our total aid effort of maximum benefit to the developing nations.

The proposals set forth above are likely to encounter resistance from many quarters. Some may say that this is exactly what has been done for some years in assistance planning. Others will argue that an integrated analysis of human resource development is too complex to be of practical usefulness. A few might question the ability of our representatives abroad to handle the task. To be sure, there are organizational and jurisdictional problems within our foreign service and foreign aid establishment. And it will be difficult, indeed, to find competent human resource specialists for a back-stopping organization.

These difficulties, however, must be weighed against the consequences of taking no steps at all. If we do not know where to go, almost any road will take us there. If we must make choices in providing from limited resources assistance to developing countries, it is necessary to establish priorities. But priorities can be established only by examination of alternatives, and this can be done best by an integrated analysis of systems which give some ordering of a vast array of facts, hunches, programs, and proposals.

My final suggestion, therefore, is to try this integrated analysis approach in three countries. We might select one in Latin America, one in Africa, and one in Asia where the United States is extensively involved in assistance both through government agencies and foundations. For each country, a task force could be organized which would be composed of experts drawn from the government, the universities and perhaps the foundations. Hopefully, with the collaboration also of the country involved, each task force would undertake a modest but integrated analysis of the system of human resource development and utilization in that country. The three task forces would thus produce some preliminary "models" to test the analytical and operational feasibility of implementing the kind of approach which has been suggested. Certainly, it would be possible to find the expert personnel from government and academia to mount a small but strategic effort of this kind. And this effort, if properly organized, could win very substantial rewards not only for the United States but also for the developing nations at large.

Commentary

Review of
the de Kiewiet Paper

**Paul R.
Hanna**

Dr. de Kiewiet begins by saying that the gates have been opened for the U.S. university community to enter into the center of U.S. foreign policy concerns. He goes on to indicate the two great themes of U.S. foreign policy, one, to prevent World War III and the other, to help fill the deficiencies in stability, in prosperity, health, and modern competence in the developing countries. The de Kiewiet paper is devoted almost exclusively to this second purpose, that is, assisting the developing nations whose people are emerging from nineteenth century colonialism. He points out that while political independence is now a legal fact, such independence without political stability in institutions and in citizens' behavior, without viable social and economic institutions is a dangerous anomaly which may be the seedbed for a major crisis. The calm accompanying the transition to independence may have lulled us into a belief that all would eventually be well if we could universally accept the Wilson proposition of universal nationhood. He goes on to point out that we have underestimated the magnitude of further steps going beyond written constitutionality, that is, the steps which are necessary for national survival and progress toward modernity. And this lag, these voids and vacuums may blow up a very devastating storm.

Dr. de Kiewiet points out also that the conquered and dispossessed people of the world who have suffered for four centuries are rewriting their own history. The Western world has lost its monopoly over the fate of what had been the colonial world. There is a major and important factor we may be overlooking in attempting to understand and deal with the newly independent and developing nations. We are prone to think in terms of our own revolutionary development, and to project similar rational growth for these nations currently rewriting their own histories. In so doing we neglect the factor of a century of intellectual maturing of both leaders and a large middle class citizenry that had taken place by the mid-eighteenth century in colonial America. This type of development is noticeably lacking in most of the newly created nations. The fundamental question then should be asked: Are there enough developed intellectual resources in many of the developing nations to provide the economic and social forward thrust to match the paper constitutions and to create a viable national community? Assuming that the answer is negative in many situations, Dr. de Kiewiet goes on to ask: What are the intellectual resources to be created to fill the voids and vacuums in the developing nations? Could part of the answer to building these resources be found in the spokesmen and leaders of the emerging societies' drawing on the ethic and the concepts readily available in British, French, and American universities? Can a joint endeavor of the leaders around the world utilizing the resources of the university system contribute to the solution of the gaps in the modernization process? Obviously, Dr. de Kiewiet does believe that part of the answer lies in this approach.

The U.S. university community has a large stake in the rational solution of the problems of U.S. foreign policy emanating from three major concerns. First, there is the intellectual concern of the scholar's searching, analyzing, and conceptualizing about foreign policy. There is also the organizational concern of both scholars and their institutions over working with government in foreign policy formation; and finally, there is an operational concern, a concern that universities carry their fair share of the responsibility for operations designed to help fill the voids and vacuums in the developing nations. The government in the strict sense is the creator of foreign policy, but this task is not satisfactorily carried by one authority alone. The process of policy formation must involve a vast task of thought, examination, and clarification. In this task the government and the scholarly community must reenforce one another. The obvious part for the university in this process will call for staff, and programs, which at the present the university does not possess in sufficient depth.

One of the deficiencies in the university arises from the rapidity with which new problems in the foreign field are generated, and the complexity of the multidimensional nature of the solutions. New fields and disciplines are needed constantly. In capsulizing, Dr. de Kiewiet says we face a task as difficult as did Rome the city when it became Rome the empire. The qualitative aspects of ever-changing foreign policy issues are almost overwhelming. Changes in curriculum must reflect the greatness of promise and the awfulness of menace that form one of the authentic watersheds of human history. Our government has clearly seen this need to invest in higher education as an important component in foreign policy decision making, both for the new knowledge and concepts as well as for the trained manpower to work with government and in government. In the developing nations, we see the striking role of the university as it plays a vital part in building a nation. These nations are investing their own institutions with a major role in the modernizing process, and the universities of the more mature nations are sustaining the process. This new role for universities has brought with it an important change in the nature of scholarship and research. No longer does a dogmatic distinction exist between pure research and applied research, between principle and practice. Thought is the thought of action, and action is the action of thought. One may speak of closing the gap between knowledge expressed in its theoretical shape and knowledge in its dynamic form. We have achieved such linkage between science and its application to the fields that draw on it, but we have yet to achieve such linkage between social sciences and humanities and their application to relations between men, nations, and cultures. The paucity of creative response from the academic community to President Johnson's request for new ideas to solve such problems as overpopulation, urbanism, racism, world law and order, is distressing to all of us. It was an invitation to the total university community to enter more fully and more creatively into solving the great issues of our time. These great issues of foreign and domestic policy make urgent the development of adequate instruments and practices of consultation, communication, and cooperation between governments and higher education. The new shared tasks demand increasing concern and activity on the part of the university, and demand long time-span and application. History shows that institution building, particularly the building of universities, is a slow process. It calls for planfulness, coordination, and interdisciplinary approaches. In short, it calls for a flexible, watchful, and constructive strategy. History also shows that the university models in the developing countries patterned after the European universities of the eighteenth and nineteenth centuries are poorly suited to the demands of modernization. Assistance in this kind of development requires first that education be seen in its wholeness, and second, that it be viewed as a primary and not just an auxiliary factor in development. We must abandon the notion that there exists a benign free market economy in education and its products.

Dr. de Kiewiet goes on to discuss the nature of planned coordination between scholarly resources of the university and the national needs for rational development. These needs require that the academic mind no longer resist a linkage between the scholarly and the structural organization and operation. Academia in the United States must assist the government in carrying out that component of foreign policy which has to do with planning educational strategies for development. In the widening relationships between universities and government there are six components to communications between the two sectors that Dr. de Kiewiet strongly emphasizes. Means of communications between government and the academic community must be organic, reliable, experienced, interested, continuous, and available. The partnership to date has been much more talked about than practiced. The fault is traceable in both partners. Universities too often fail to carry out their responsibilities overseas in an effective way. Their representatives are sometimes not as competent as we would hope. Unless the heart of the academic community at home takes seriously this partnership abroad, no administrative commitment will alone turn the trick. Little profit will result for the developing nation being assisted, and even less profit will flow back to become a permanent resource of the U.S. university. These errors need correcting. A valuable legacy of permanent intellectual and institutional bonds, exchanges, and even interdependence should be planfully prepared to follow the relationships which exist in assistance activities.

After Dr. de Kiewiet had thought further about his thesis, he added these remarks:

I felt the need to remove some of the complacency about the new countries and to assail the unrealistic assumption that political independence was a real, solid, and stable achievement. Without the realization that this assumption is false, the effort to build up the new nations is deprived of its deep and grim necessity. The whole paper is intentionally broad so as to develop a broad range for response. I hope it will stimulate a wide range of response on the closeness of the university to national problems. Purists will not like this notion, but the unrealism of ivory tower pure research needs to be exposed. It is important to recognize and advance the proposition that the social sciences are moving and must be helped to move into a relationship where they can work with strength and purpose on domestic and national issues. Without suggesting any rivalry with science I feel the social sciences on a discriminatory basis require the financial and organizational support that science has had and used so very effectively. I should like to stress these three issues. The first deals with the imperative need, if new

61

funds are to become available, to put them to the service of the university as an academic community and not as a fiscal body. I am quite sure that the distortions and defects in university contracts that have occurred have been caused by those university officials acting in the capacity for the academicians. These administrative officials can no longer give major attention to the innovative intellectual opportunities of the present generation. Government officials can deal more efficiently with the fiscal officers, and so the contracts have been devices and mechanisms with too little inspiration and ferment from within the academic community contributing to the planning.

I would again emphasize the vital need for a properly organized, reasonable dialogue between the government and the academic community on how to use academic personnel and resources abroad. And I am not in favor of the contract mechanism. Thirdly, I am deeply serious about the unity of all education, and am opposed to university compartmentalization. The interdisciplinary emphasis is paramount.

Dr. de Kiewiet has put his finger on one of the most crucial issues, and that is the false notion of the separateness of each of the disciplines and departments and professional schools. What we need is a more wholistic attack on major problems at home and abroad. Dr. de Kiewiet is saying there should no longer be a separation but rather a unity and a supplementation of the government and academic community and for a marriage of research, knowledge, and its application. There is a need for scholars and professional schools to thrust their research tools deep into the living tissue of major social and economic problems in order to discover the most crucial principles of their disciplines and to test the reliability of these principles. The need is to link knowledge with policy decision making. And we need also to redress a long standing debt which we owe for several centuries of educational assistance we have received from older nations.

My last point has to do with what I consider an overemphasis on the binational and an underemphasis on the multinational approach to our relationships with other nations. I fully understand our governmental policy of maintaining the flexibility to work binationally or multinationally, but it seems to me the realities of the future will be far more caught up in the development of multinational, regional patterns which are now emerging.

Commentary
Review of
the Harbison Paper

At the outset Dr. Harbison makes two assumptions about U.S. technical assistance activities abroad. First, an objective of U.S. foreign policy is to help accelerate social and economic development in the less developed parts of the world. A goal of that policy is to devote limited financial resources to assist these less developed countries and to use these resources in such a way as to make the maximum contribution to the economic and social development of the countries assisted. The second assumption is that the capacity to develop economically and socially will depend on the country's ability to develop and utilize its human resources. U.S. aid has stressed educational development, and the university-to-university contract relationship has been and will continue to be an effective means of assistance. Dr. Harbison points out, nonetheless, that there has been dereliction on the part of university contractors, that American staffs have been of questionable competence, and that the university commitment to long-range development has been too limited. University efforts have also contributed to the brain drain from the underdeveloped countries, he asserts.

Royden C. Dangerfield

Finally, Dr. Harbison concludes that the honeymoon stage in technical assistance is over. It is now time for the United States to rethink its programs, to shape them so that they meet the needs of the assisted countries more realistically and also fit within our own capabilities more realistically. It is now time to think through carefully a concept of strategy building based upon the examination of alternatives and the choice of priorities.

It is clear, Dr. Harbison states, that political and social pressures are now forcing the developing countries to commit ever increasing proportions of their resources to education, so the crucial problem is to find ways for these countries to derive greater social and economic benefit from their investment. In short, they have got to get a greater return from the training of their human resources. Too often these countries have stressed quantity over quality, and Dr. Harbison regrets this. Also, they have tended to

63

deal exclusively with high-level manpower requirements when they need lower-level manpower resources. Dr. Harbison analyzes the pattern of need in these terms: In the typical underdeveloped country, the general system of human resource utilization can best be understood by an integrative analysis of five component systems. He labels these: (1) employment generation, (2) formal education, (3) training and development in employment, (4) movements of manpower with critical skills, and (5) planning and strategy development. As economies develop, they create opportunities for people to engage in productive activities which hopefully increase their real wealth and the wealth of the nation. The system seldom works perfectly, but this is dependent upon the form development takes. There are shortages of persons with critical skills, shortages of persons with knowledge, and a surplus of people seeking opportunities which the economy cannot provide. The second system is that of formal education, and here the bridging from an older to a modern society constitutes a real problem in terms of education. In the developing countries opportunities for education are limited, and thus it is important to determine who may have access to the opportunities that do exist. The orientation of the educational system is important, whether it is oriented toward higher education, designed to educate the masses, or to generate an elite. Is vocational education intended to generate specific skills or to provide reasonably broad pre-employment education? Several choices must be made regarding the nature of the formal educational system.

Dr. Harbison goes on to discuss in-service or on-the-job training. Specific training is largely the responsibility of the employing institutions; therefore it is important to view this training as a distinct system, separate, but hopefully closely connected to, the formal educational system. The author discusses the movement of manpower with critical skills, then he points out the great need which he dwells on throughout the paper, and that is the need for planning, for the building of a strategy for the development of human resources. To achieve this strategy Dr. Harbison has some concrete proposals. First, he asks whether it is possible to build the competence and machinery for an integrated analysis of systems of human resource development and utilization in other countries as a basis for foreign policy. This is a typical economist's question, and he answers it affirmatively.

After answering affirmatively, Dr. Harbison points out that a framework must be created for undertaking such an integrated analysis, and that information will be difficult to obtain in many instances. He suggests however that a back-stopping organization, not necessarily governmental, be created to provide the information base needed for an integrated analysis. He sees the organization as having no responsibility for policy but merely providing the bases for decision making by the U.S. representatives in the country being considered. He thinks also that the International Education Act might provide funds to support research in universities to produce the kind of basic knowledge about the development and utilization of human resources that is needed. He recommends that the American academic community seize the opportunity it now has to participate in the formulation of U.S. foreign policy in the vital area of strategy building. He points out that in the past U.S. academic institutions have been asked to undertake particular assignments in particular countries. Seldom have they understood the relationship of their work to a broader plan of assistance. On the contrary, academics have assumed, quite naïvely, that someone in high office somewhere had a logical strategy in mind, and that their activity fitted within that pattern. Such has not always been the case.

U.S. institutions have the competence, and are in a position to get the resources, to assist, and in some cases, to lead a movement for a more systematic analysis of strategy building in this area of foreign policy, Dr. Harbison believes. He warns that universities and their faculties should not always hide under the umbrella of research leaving it to others to judge the usefulness and the relevance of the issues of the day. Proposals set forth in this thesis will encounter resistance from many quarters. Some will say we have been doing exactly what he is recommending here for years. Others will argue that an integrated analysis of human resource development is too complex to be useful. A few will question the ability of U.S. representatives abroad to handle such a task. Dr. Harbison recognizes all of these difficulties and argues that if we must make choices in providing assistance to developing countries, with limited resources, it is necessary to set priorities. Priorities can only be set by an examination of alternatives, and this can best be done by an integrated analysis that gives some order to a vast array of facts, hunches, programs, and proposals. Dr. Harbison makes one final suggestion that the United States establish a task force for one country in which we are heavily involved in assistance programs for each major developing area, one for Asia, for Africa, and for Latin America, each to make an integrated analysis as he has proposed. Each team should include experts from universities, government, and perhaps from the foundations. The three task forces could establish some models by which to test the operational feasibility for the kind of approach he has proposed.

Anyone who has been involved in the technical assistance contracts the universities have carried out has been aware of the fact that the pluralism of the university has been a handicap in the execution of the contract—and also aware that the kind of staff member who will go abroad is not always the man who is most pressingly needed. One is also aware that the contract affects a professional school involved, but does not necessarily have any effect on the entire university. One is aware too that there are inherent difficulties in recruiting the right kind of men. Dr. Harbison would argue that if we had a model, if we had a strategy, we might be able to overcome some of these handicaps we all know to exist in technical assistance activities.

Commentary
Summary of
the Discussion

Discussion following the de Kiewiet and Harbison papers focussed on the complexities involved in accomplishing objectives proposed by the authors: the complexity of organizing the university as an entity; the complexity of the government's activities and problems; and finally, the complexity of the relationships between the two in undertaking operations of an international educational nature.

Elizabeth N.
Shiver

Seminar Chairman Stephen K. Bailey posed several questions regarding the organization of an institution *vis a vis* the de Kiewiet and Harbison proposals:

How do we move from what we know our universities to be (as institutions) at least in the direction of the goals suggested by Dr. de Kiewiet? How do we attempt within the university structure to become responsive to policy questions where the need is to develop patient analyses, and to develop fertile hypotheses which can help explain our observations and help define viable possibilities in terms of policy alternatives? This is an extraordinarily complex undertaking. So far our ability to develop within our university system mechanisms to examine cross-cutting questions, to develop responsible enthusiasms which have some focus, has been severely limited. I submit that the university's difficulties in dealing with these complexities is a microcosm of the total problem.

If we really understood the process of linking the methodological and analytical niceties of modern life, if we understood how a university administration can attempt to link several diverse fields into only a loose confederation for the purposes of conducting the kind of colloquy that has been proposed, then perhaps we could unlock some doors in understanding the complex relationships between universities as a whole and government agencies, individually and as a total structure, and also universities' relationships to

67

agencies and government abroad. Professor Harbison's approach to an over-all analysis of human resource development provides an example of the kind of confederation that is needed within the institution itself. To cite an incomplete list, participation would be needed from the departments of economics, demography, medicine, public health, political science, education, anthropology, sociology, even religion.

It is possible that the main problem is to ascertain which parts of the institution are relevant to the question at hand, which parts of the institution must be taken into account for any specific problem. It is doubtful that we will ever reach the point of being able to deal with "an institution" in the complex sense, especially an institution such as a university which attracts the individuals who comprise it, to a large extent, because it tends to leave them alone. There is a complex set of tensions here between the reality of an educational institution and the objectives we are seeking to meet in foreign policy.

The Seminar questioned at the outset certain assumptions made in the de Kiewiet and Harbison papers about the role of educational institutions in development assistance abroad. It was suggested that the filling of voids and vacuums in developing nations is a process designed to promote political stability, and further, that the promotion of stability is a political objective appropriate to the government, but not necessarily appropriate to educational institutions. The Seminar also noted that, granting institutional willingness to participate in development assistance, much was still unknown about stimulating the process of change in developing nations. Objections were also raised to Professor Harbison's proposal for an integrated analysis of needs in relation to resources on grounds that the proposal can be construed as an arrogant posture, an assumption that methods of decision making can be applied in developing nations which have never been applied in the United States and which are perhaps unworkable wherever there is a free political process.

Nevertheless, it was argued, American education (as well as science, technology, and industry) is so heavily involved overseas that it is pointless to argue whether it should be, and that the involvement with United States foreign policy goals is inescapable. Further, any move in the direction of greater rationality and improved planning in resource development abroad is a step in the right direction, irrespective of the state of comparable planning in the United States itself.

It was suggested further that Professor Harbison's goal was a kind of informational and conceptual infrastructure which could be helpful in the decision-making process. Even though policies and plans have been developed to a degree through chance interaction, there are rational elements which have been infused and can increasingly be infused in the decision-making process to reduce at least the margin for error. To develop sounder knowledge of needs and resources is not to deny or negate political processes.

Consideration was given to practical steps that can be taken in the organization of the university to meet public service demands in the international area. It was emphasized that many universities are in fact prepared to act, prepared to respond to requests for services they are especially able to provide. Universities are uniquely qualified in some situations. Certain factors begin to be self-evident as an institution comes to define its role and responsibilities in public international service. First, there needs to be a correlation among the several segments of international activity within an institution. The international interests of the institution should be pervasive rather than isolated. This tenet requires that there be an organic connection between curricular development, faculty and student exchange programs, library and resource development, and overseas study and research projects as well as technical assistance. Second, no one institution, nor one part of a multi-institution, can attempt to undertake everything there is to be done in the international area. The total resources of an institution, or a state or area, need to be considered in such a way that they will be complementary and reenforcing. Third, the institution must move to take practical steps toward solving immediate problems resulting from involvement in overseas activities. Finally, the faculty must be involved in setting policies. One participant encapsulated in the following way:

> We are learning that the organic approach is essential, that the distribution of emphasis is essential, that the organization of the university's resources is essential, and that the policies to be developed must involve deeply and radically the faculty across the board, and they must in turn be integrated with administrative decision making so that whatever we ultimately achieve carries the whole university forward in its academic program as well as in research, teaching, and public service.

The Seminar was in general agreement that the social sciences are the area most in need of attention within the academic community in relation to the proposals of de Kiewiet and Harbison.

Specifically, the social sciences need far greater support if they are to serve as instruments useful in meeting the problems the authors described. Both within the government and without, there was thought to be substantial agreement that the social sciences need sustained support, but there was no firm agreement on what form such support should take. The concept of a government-supported National Science Foundation was not unanimously endorsed. There is a question of determining how much support the social sciences are presently receiving as well as the question of how much support is actually needed. There is also the problem of determining whether a special mechanism is needed to channel federal support. Opposing arguments are that such a special mechanism would be a peculiarly visible and vulnerable operation, subject to controversy and criticism if it were doing its proper job. A certain amount of dispersal of support and activities may serve all concerned in a more constructive way.

It was pointed out also that the humanities have a very definite contribution to make to international educational development that should not be overlooked. The humanities add wisdom to technical know-how, they broaden the base of the elite, they are as responsible for the quality of a nation's life as are the social sciences. The de Kiewiet paper points to the false expectation that an instant constitution can create a stable society. The American Constitution grew out of a century of thought and debate, grounded in philosophy, knowledge of man, and human experience for which literature, history, and the arts were the vehicle.

More general support for international activities was discussed in part in relation to the International Education Act and its purposes. It was pointed out that the background papers generally spoke in terms of the International Education Act's serving as a substitute for other funds or an additional source of funds for aiding overseas activities whereas the language of the Act clearly states that it is intended to support infusion of international studies into the domestic university structure. Assistant Secretary for Education Paul Miller of the Department of Health, Education, and Welfare, was asked specifically to comment on this point. He said:

> It is easy to understand how one might view the International Education Act as a substitute measure for some kind of large, mission-oriented activity. The purposes of the Act are in fact domestic, but having said that, I think it is very cogent to our discussions to recognize that as you build strength domestically within an institution, you increase its

competence to perform overseas technical assistance activities, and to engage in other kinds of overseas activities of its own. There is a connection here, and I do not think we must view the development of these various competencies as completely separate. They will become mutually supportive.

The Seminar turned its attention also to the problems the government has in dealing with universities as institutions. The complexity of the university makes it difficult for the government to identify central and concrete responsibility within the institution, that is, to know where to turn. While academics complain that the government tends to deal too much through administrative officers who do not understand the requirements of the programs with which they are working, for its part the government is groping to find its way through the institutions' organizational maze. The government's basic problem is to find some way to deal with universities as universities. All too often relationships between government and institutions are in fact only relationships between two individuals with the university serving as an umbrella. The government is now turning its attention to working with institutions as institutions. It hopes to strengthen institutional relationships in a way that will be more beneficial both to the government and the university.

There was some debate over the difference (or lack of difference) in dealing with institutions and with individuals, whether in fact an institution can be considered anything more than a collection of individuals with widely disparate interests. There was concern over the shift in government emphasis to the institutional approach, concern for what the change would mean to the academic community. On the other hand the shift to institutional emphasis was also seen as a commendable effort, one that should benefit the university. The shift in approach is at present primarily in the exchange programs open to individuals. Assistant Secretary of State Charles Frankel explained the new approach:

> We are not wedded to the proposition that one can neatly separate an individual and an institutional approach. Obviously these are two foci for looking at a set of problems. Primarily we are talking about a system of selection of individuals for exchange programs which will ask certain new questions. One question would be the relation of the individual's project to educational plans and priorities in the United States and in the other country. We are

71

agreed that all individuals cannot and should not fit into some predetermined plan or some set of priorities. There are individuals who have talent who are worth encouraging whether or not they fit some administrative design. Nonetheless, to allow a margin for individuals and choose perhaps a third of the exchangees for their own merits alone is in itself a deliberate and rational plan.

Other than the promotion of individual talent, however, we are thinking in terms of assigning individuals in such a way to develop a continuing pattern of institutional involvement, a pattern of self-sustaining and mutually supportive activities between both the institutions and the individuals within them. While individuals have gone out and profited from their experiences as they should, our exchange programs have suffered from the fact that these individuals have not been fitted into patterns of ongoing activities, either in their own institutions or in relation to their foreign institutions. Another objective is to assure that educational advantages will accrue to the institution from the individual's experience, that there is a possibility of some effect on research, curricula, and interdisciplinary efforts. Simply put, we hope to select people in such a way as to assure regular follow-up effect after the exchange period. I think that we will have a better basis, a better rationale, for what we are attempting to do in exchange programs than we do if we only talk about increasing exchanges for the sake of exchanges.

Government, the Universities, and International Affairs:
A Crisis in Identity *

THE MALAISE

THE PROBLEM OF IDENTITY

Psychologists tell us that identity is the nucleus of the individual's belief system, which serves, in turn, as his blueprint for relating to his physical and social environment. When it is lost, the individual finds it difficult to live with himself, or to adapt to the reality around him. If he is ever to function viably, he must find the answers to three related questions: (1) "Who am I?" (2) "What is the nature of the society and of the world in which I live?" (3) "How can I relate to it?" The restoration of lost identity is of crucial importance to personal survival.[1]

Walter Adams and Adrian Jaffe

Organizations and social institutions also require a clear sense of identity. Without it, they can no more function effectively than can individuals. If they are to play a purposeful role in conjunction with others, if they are to relate meaningfully to society and to other institutions, they must preserve their identity by keeping intact an unambiguous system of beliefs. They must, in short, know who they are, and they must have a continuing commitment to an integral system of values.

IDENTITY AND THE AMERICAN UNIVERSITY

The loss by the American university of a sense of its identity reached serious proportions at the time that it became, in Clark Kerr's felicitous phrase, a "multiversity." But the process had been going on for a long time, and many of its aspects were inherent in

* Preparation of this paper was supported by the American Council on Education and the U.S. Advisory Commission on International Educational and Cultural Affairs. The Advisory Commission, created under the Fulbright-Hays Act of 1961, is charged with sending reports pertinent to international exchange activities to the Congress. It has submitted this paper to the Congress as an Advisory Commission document, and the Committee on Foreign Affairs has issued it as House Document 120.

[1] See Milton Rokeach, "The Three Christs of Ypsilanti," New York: Alfred A. Knopf, 1964, pp. 19–36, 311–18.

the nature of the institution itself: an organization of individuals whose primary purpose is to interact in order to change each other, the state of knowledge, and society itself. The university—"a community that thinks," as Robert Hutchins put it—rests on the assumption that society requires an organization which is engaged in a continuous search and conversation "aimed at truth." [2]

As early as the eighteenth century, however, men like Thomas Jefferson and Benjamin Rush recognized that education must serve the community in practical ways, and that the university could not be an ivory tower removed from the world of action. On the contrary, since anything worth thinking about has consequences in the practical order, the university had to be involved in the world, and not separate. This understanding, and conviction, was shared in the nineteenth century by university presidents such as Eliot of Harvard and Gilman of Johns Hopkins, as well as by their colleagues in the State universities and the land-grant colleges, and in our own time by John Dewey and Alfred North Whitehead, who insisted that "celibacy does not suit a university. It must mate itself with action."

THE CONSEQUENCES OF INVOLVEMENT

In its effort to "mate itself with action," the American university has displayed organizational skill and operational flair. It has offered itself as possessing certain special attributes which serve to make its services attractive to potential clients in Government and industry. Turning its unique characteristics to advantage and losing sight of the original role of the "community that thinks," the university proclaimed its "capacity to move swiftly, flexibly, and imaginatively into a new area of critical need: the power to arrive at a disinterested, objective appraisal of a situation free of political influence; the freedom to engage in controversial activities; the ability to experiment in an unfettered manner—and if need be fail; and finally the capacity for sympathetic personal attention to the variety of human problems that beset our increasingly dehumanized world." [3] The university converted its natural mandate to participate in society into an eager solicitation of clientele, and in the process not only became a "multiversity," but began to forget what it was, what it served, and what its belief system consisted of.

[2] "The University of Utopia," Chicago: University of Chicago Press, 1953, pp. 41, 56.
[3] Cp. Carnegie Corp. of New York, Annual Report, 1966, p. 7, in re nongovernmental organizations.

In its increasing reliance upon "outsiders" to buy its services and to support its projects the university found an effective means of cementing its organic integration into contemporary society, but this was neither painless nor free from serious cost. Ancient bonds were broken, traditional relationships were shattered, and customary functions were transmuted. The need to serve many clients often resulted in the neglect of the original clients, the students; the primary conception of the university as an "instrument of rationality . . . dedicated to reason" became blurred under the weight of conflicting pressures.[4] The introduction into the university of new systems of values was confusing; the natural dualism of the university's role, instead of being a source of strength, became a source of ambiguity and hence of weakness. The continuing sense of selfhood was lost, and with it there often came, as in human schizophrenia, a frantic denial of the old symbols and a baffled, random, and ineffective assumption of a large and unsatisfactory range of *ad hoc* roles.

As it began increasingly to relate to coordinate but divergent segments of society, the university tended to abandon its traditional guidelines without finding new ones of relevance. "Wavering between the profit and the loss, in this brief transit where the dreams cross," the university moved toward a future of greater, not lesser problems—problems of identity. In the words of John Gardner, ". . . as industry and government, with their huge research and education programs, come to look more and more like universities, and as the universities with their worldly interests come to look more and more like the rest of society, we shall achieve a condition in which no one will be quite sure what is university and what is nonuniversity, and no one will have the faintest idea what is organized around what." [5]

The illness which Gardner predicted has already infected the patient. We can call it "crisis of identity," which it certainly is; it is useful, however, to examine some of the symptoms.

THE SYMPTOMS

THE BEGINNINGS

The crisis of identity, like so many illnesses, had innocent and understandable origins. Although it has brought about a serious condition at present, the relationship between Government and the universities, in its early form, was of formidable benefit to

[4] See e.g., George G. Stern, "Myth and Reality in the American College," AAUP Bulletin, December 1966.
[5] John W. Gardner, "The Future of the University," Saturday Review, vol. 46, No. 2, 1963, p. 46.

both. No responsible educator can fail to acknowledge the enormous debt which universities have to Government for their growth, their ability to provide education to increasingly large numbers of students, and for their capacity to engage in important research. Nor would any governmental official wish to deny the great extent to which university cooperation has been beneficial to the country's interests.

At the close of World War II, the desire of the universities actively to engage in the practical world coincided with the needs of Government to a remarkable degree. The Government wished to avoid building large in-house facilities for research; it wanted to farm it out to fiscally responsible institutions which had existing facilities and demonstrated capabilities; it wanted to give these tasks to nonprofit, noncontroversial organizations which would help it to avoid congressional criticism. For their part, the universities did not want the Government to build in-house facilities which might compete with them or draw talent from the campuses; they did not want university talent to flow into governmental organizations like Rand, from which there would be no direct feedback to the instructional programs. In addition, the universities wanted a source of funds for the kind of basic research which they knew had to be done, but which could not be supported from relatively meager internal resources. It was, in short, a marriage of almost perfect convenience, and one which has worked remarkably well, producing often spectacular results.

The relationship between Government and universities, however, grew in a topsy-turvy fashion which brought about some fundamental problems and highlighted some points of danger. Many of these have been identified by responsible critics of the Government-university contract system, and may be regarded, in this context, as symptomatic of the organic disease. Although they differ in scope, all of the criticisms have in common the implicit confusion of belief systems and the consequent confusion of roles besetting both partners. The criticisms fall into a number of general patterns.

THE COMPLIANCE OF THE UNIVERSITIES

If the Government has offered various blandishments to the universities to engage in contractual projects, the universities, like Barkis, have been "willin'." The French put it well in their saying, "chose que plaît est à demi vendue," but even more succinct is this limerick written by Don K. Price, dean of the John F. Kennedy School of Government at Harvard:

There was a young lady from Kent,
Who said that she knew what it meant,
When men took her to dine
Gave her cocktails and wine
She knew what it meant—but she went.[6]

In the same vein, Richard M. Morse, professor of history at Yale University and chairman of its Latin American studies, underscores the essentially passive posture of universities in responding to extramural Government initiatives. Morse writes:

> American universities, often ensconced on comfortable land grants, have been singularly docile in taking leads from the Federal Government. They never bite the hand that feeds; at best they glower before eating. They dutifully produce atom bombs and Tagalog speakers. When the chill winds of McCarthyism blow from Washington, they philosophically hunch their shoulders against them. When the calls to New Frontiers and Great Societies are issued, they respond with cautious sympathy.[7]

This receptivity to outside stimuli—this willingness to become a Federal grant university—is especially marked in the international field. As John Gardner told the American Council on Education some 8 years ago:

> When a Government agency with money to spend approaches a university it can usually purchase almost any service it wants. . . . When the International Cooperation Administration began to write contracts with the universities for overseas service, it conceived the relationship as basically a purchase of services, and unfortunately many universities acquiesced. A good many of the universities did not ask whether the activities in question . . . were a wise expenditure of effort in terms of the total mission of the university, whether they would leave any increment of growth for the institution itself.
>
> One may criticize the ICA for using the universities in this fashion. But as long as the universities have no concep-

[6] Quoted in Clark Kerr, "The Uses of the University," Cambridge: Harvard University Press, 1964, p. 69.

[7] Paper presented at Conference on Foreign Language and Area Studies, Princeton University, December 17–18, 1965; reprinted in "International Education: Past, Present, Problems and Prospects," House Document No. 527, 89th Cong., 2d sess., 1966, p. 171 (hereinafter cited as "Brademas Compendium").

tion of themselves other than the supermarket conception, they will have to resign themselves to the fact that people will walk in off the street, buy a box of Wheaties, and walk out.[8]

This relationship between an interested Government and a compliant university results not so much, as many fear, in Government control and domination, as in Government influence. As Clark Kerr, until recently president of the University of California, expressed it:

The real problem is not one of Federal control but of Federal influence. A Federal agency offers a project. The university need not accept, but as a practical matter, it usually does. . . . Out of this reality have followed many of the consequences of Federal aid for the universities; and they have been substantial. That they are subtle, slowly cumulative, and gentlemanly makes them all the more potent.[9]

THE UNIVERSITY AS MENDICANT

These criticisms direct attention to the general passive willingness of universities to accept what is offered to them, but this passivity is matched by an extremely active program of seeking out grants and projects. As a seeker of grants, the university, like commercial firms with products to sell, uses aggressive advertisement in the promotion of its wares and in some cases has not only a series of professional promoters on campus, but an office in Washington as well. The president of the University of Rochester, W. Allen Wallis, observes in this connection that—

. . . universities, besides trying to preserve their traditional role, have become important wheelers and dealers in affairs large and small. They accept, indeed seek, assignments (if accompanied by funds) from businesses, governments, foundations, or individuals to carry out specified missions on stated schedules. At times, they even agree to keep the results secret, for the exclusive benefit of the client. Only a little money they accept . . . is for purposes as broad as those traditionally associated with universities.[10]

[8] "The University in Our Civilization," reprinted in "Brademas Compendium," pp. 41, 44.
[9] Kerr, op. cit., pp. 57–58.
[10] "Centripetal and Centrifugal Forces in University Organization," in Robert S. Morrison (ed.), "The Contemporary University: U.S.A.," Boston: Houghton Mifflin, 1966, p. 41.

As a result, concludes Wallis, the university's role is "in danger of becoming something like that of hotelkeeper for transient scholars and projects." [11]

The zealous pursuit of grants by the mendicant university has another unfortunate result: the development on the campuses of marginal personnel, distinct from the traditional faculty, whose exclusive skills are in the grant-handling processes and who frequently negotiate contracts and commit their institutions without the involvement or the consent, and often without the knowledge, of the faculty directly and professionally concerned. The lack of faculty involvement in the phases of contract negotiation explains why, on most university campuses, Government projects are almost totally segregated from the academic enterprise of the university, to which they stand in the relationship of a sideshow. Paul A. Miller, former president of the University of West Virginia, and now Assistant Secretary of Health, Education, and Welfare, remarks, for example, that—

> . . . the new programs in international affairs tend to be assigned to discrete and recently established units. . . . Technical assistance projects, while drawing on departmental competence, are negotiated, contracted, staffed, and evaluated by special offices and personnel.[12]

Apart from the inappropriateness, on campuses, of this new and extensive class of ancillaries, they pose another serious problem. While within the academic profession it is not difficult to distinguish between the professional and the nonprofessional, the distinction is seldom clear to persons in other fields, who assume, quite understandably, that everybody on a campus is part of the "faculty," and doing about the same sort of thing. This assumption is made more likely when the same titles and ranks are shared by all, regardless of primary function. It thus often happens that Government, for example, may be under the impression that it has the approval of the entire university, and its wholehearted support, when in fact it may have the approval of only a special group of administrative officers who neither know nor consider the wishes of the professorial staff in the older sense of the term. Such a situation serves not only to make a reasonable dialog harder; it often produces acute embarrassment and serious misunderstanding.

[11] Ibid., p. 46.
[12] "The Role of the University in Developing World Community," reprinted in Brademas Compendium, p. 65.

Robert M. Rosenzweig, associate dean of the graduate division at Stanford University, is well aware of this situation. "One of the dismal sights in American higher education," he writes,

> is that of administrators scrambling for contracts for work which does not emerge from the research or teaching interests of their faculty. The result of this unseemly enterprise is bound to be a faculty coerced or seduced into secondary lines of interest, or a frantic effort to secure nonfaculty personnel to meet the contractual obligations. Among the most puzzling aspects of such arrangements is the fact that Government agencies have permitted and even encouraged them. Not only are they harmful to the universities—which is not, of course, the Government's prime concern—but they insure that the Government will not get what it is presumably buying; namely, the intellectual and technical resources of the academic community. It is simply a bad bargain all the way around.[13]

Dean Rosenzweig might have gone on to point out that many of the nonfaculty personnel who are thus recruited end up with faculty rank, making it impossible thereafter to identify or to distinguish them. This may be one of the reasons why Government seems to have encouraged this sort of arrangement; while it certainly is Government's concern that universities should not be harmed, it has no reason to question the internal operation of a university, nor does it have the knowledge or the vocabulary; if it is fooled, it is no more so than the large numbers of people who assume that he who wears a white coat is a physician.

THE SHORT-CHANGING OF GOVERNMENT

Since it is only seldom that external projects become an integral and coherent part of the *academic* community, the Government does not get what it thinks it is buying, and what it often pays for most generously: the technical and intellectual resources which the university, in theory, is supposed to supply. It is, to put it bluntly, short-changed, and no one who has the country's interests at heart can look at this without regret and alarm. The eagerness of university administrations to undertake stylized, Government-financed projects has caused a decline in self-generated commitments to scholarly pursuits, has produced baneful effects on the academic mission of our universities, and has, in addition, brought forward

[13] "Universities and the Foreign Assistance Program," Journal of Higher Education, October 1964; reprinted in "Brademas Compendium," p. 432.

some bitter complaints from the disappointed clients. According to one reliable report, the Agency for International Development claims that—

> . . . universities have often acted irresponsibly—sending third-rate personnel overseas, neglecting the needs of the host country while they concentrate on what *they* want to do, engaging in aggressive tactics to get contracts, taking on tasks they are not equipped to do. . . . Some AID officials add that no U.S. university ever willingly terminated a contract program, no matter how valid the reasons for doing so.[14]

Some of these charges are exaggerated and the denunciation is too sweeping; yet they tend to suggest that from the Government's point of view, the university contract system, as presently operated, is not by any means the most satisfactory way for an agency to accomplish its mission and to discharge its responsibilities. William J. Nagle, former Director of the Office of External Research of the Department of State, finds the Government-university contract system a defective instrument for serving the needs either of Government or of the total society. He observes a singular tendency on the part of American social scientists to permit operations to dominate purposes and to refuse to act, perhaps in the hope of landing future contracts, as "responsible critics of Government policy." He finds them unwilling or unable to challenge conventional wisdom or to question some of the myths on which some aspects of policy might be based. Nagle puts it this way:

> Although I spent my three years at State in a sincere and sometimes spirited defense of our own and of other agencies' contract research programs, I must admit that there were very few of the more than 40 studies contracted during my tenure there that really proved very useful to the Department's policymakers or even to the Department's researchers. . . . Most contract researchers whose products came across my desk failed to meet the standards and needs of the Government or the academy. . . . I began to worry that I, a contract research administrator, was in fact contributing very little either to the needs of Government or to the larger society's pursuit of knowledge and truth.[15]

[14] John W. Gardner, "A.I.D. and the Universities," Washington: Agency for International Development, April 1964, p. 5.
[15] Address to the International Studies Association, Wayne State University, May 5, 1966; reprinted in "Brademas Compendium," p. 315.

Nagle reports that his disappointment and disenchantment with the contributions of academia was shared by some of the most sensitive and capable officials in Washington. Daniel P. Moynihan, an architect, when he was Assistant Secretary of Labor, of the domestic Great Society programs, was most unhappy at the poverty of ideas from the universities. Richard Goodwin, before leaving the White House, was disheartened by academia's answers to the "crisis of American public life." And Arthur Barber, Deputy Assistant Secretary of Defense, devoted an entire speech to the Washington chapter of the International Studies Association to "the failure of American intellectuals to contribute new ideas to American foreign policy. I believe the potential for courageous, intelligent intellectuals concerned with political affairs . . . has never been greater, but the response has been inadequate to the challenge."[16] What Julien Benda called the "treason" of the intellectuals may be taking the form, thirty-five years later, of the "failure" of the academic community.

THE ETHICS OF SPONSORED RESEARCH

It is largely, but not exclusively, in projects involving overseas research that an ethical problem arises and intrudes. Questions of ethics are often swept under the rug, but they have a way of coming out again in the course of time, and Project Camelot is a case in point. Camelot was a $6,000,000 research project sponsored by the U.S. Army under the aegis of an accredited American university. It involved the highly flammable subjects of counterrevolution and counterinsurgency in Latin America, and was, in effect, an effort to use "software" research in support of, or as a substitute for, "hardware" systems.

In response to criticisms in the Department of State, the Congress, and the academic community, Secretary of Defense McNamara eventually canceled the project. The reasons for the cancellation are less important than the question which the project raised of the propriety, in the first place, of the acceptance by a university of an assignment under the specified conditions and terms. Prof. Irving Louis Horowitz, of Washington University, reports:

One of the cloudiest aspects to Project Camelot is the role of (the contracting university). Its actual supervision of the contract appears to have begun and ended with the twenty-five percent overhead on those parts of the contract that a university receives on most Federal grants . . . . From

[16] Cited ibid., p. 317.

the outset, there seems to have been a "gentleman's agreement" not to inquire or interfere in Project Camelot, but simply to serve as some sort of camouflage.[17]

That "the relationship between sponsors and researchers was not one of equals, but rather one of superordinate military needs and subordinate academic roles" did not appear to trouble the contracting university nor cause it any *crise de conscience*. That the Army was "respectful and protective of free expression" seemed to be a sufficient condition for undertaking the contract. Nonetheless, in Horowitz' view, this left a fundamental ethical question unresolved:

> The propriety of the Army to define and delimit all questions, which Camelot should have had a right to examine, was never placed in doubt. This is a tragic precedent; it reflects the arrogance of a consumer of intellectual merchandise. And this relationship of inequality corrupted the lines of authority, and profoundly limited the autonomy of the social scientists involved. It became clear that the social scientist savant was not so much functioning as an applied social scientist as he was supplying information to a powerful client . . . . The sponsorship of a project, whether by the U.S. Army or by the Boy Scouts of America, is by itself neither good nor bad. Sponsorship is good or bad only insofar as the intended outcomes can be predetermined and the parameters of those intended outcomes tailored to the sponsor's expectations.[18]

In fact, the issue is pragmatic as well as ethical. A project which lacks inherent intellectual or scientific validity is not worthy of a university's effort; but at the same time the results of such a project will fail to give to its sponsor the value he paid for. The Government is shortchanged, and the university is compromised. The corruption and impoverishment of society's value system is not only deplorable in itself, but quite in vain.

The gist of these criticisms can be found in the conclusion of Clark Kerr, that American universities have "always responded, but seldom so quickly as today, to the desires and demands of external groups—sometimes for love, sometimes for gain, increasingly willingly, and, in some cases, too eagerly." [19] And however eager or willing the response may have been, it has been such as

[17] "The Life and Death of Project Camelot," Trans-Action, November-December 1965; reprinted in "Brademas Compendium," p. 298.
[18] Ibid., p. 301.
[19] Kerr, op. cit., p. 94.

to call the whole relationship of Government and universities into question, to cast doubt upon the integrity of some institutions and their faculties, to open the educational functions of universities to the arrows of Philistines, and to suggest the possibility to a world—never adverse to prejudice—that academic honesty is no less marketable than a box of detergent on the grocery shelf.

DIAGNOSIS

PRAGMATIC VERSUS IDEALISTIC INSTITUTIONS

The failure of the universities to continue their traditional functions and to reaffirm their traditional ideals has led to an unusually keen sense of despair, in good measure because of the general appreciation of the fact that they are special kinds of institutions, idealistic rather than pragmatic. It offends us that they should "sell" their services—and, perhaps, themselves.

Most institutions are necessarily pragmatic, devoted to the achievement of certain important purposes—the production of goods, the defense of the realm, the provision of medical care. As pragmatic institutions, they may be judged in accordance with how effectively they operate. If they fail to provide what they are designed to provide, they may be modified or abolished. In this context, the "good" institution is the one which works; the "bad" institution is the one which does not. "Pragmatic" is not, however, a pejorative adjective: pragmatic institutions function to make possible the environment in which people live; they are the operative structures of social organization.

Some institutions, though, are designed to accomplish another order of result, an order which relates to a transcendental system of values. These institutions, notably the educational and the religious, are concerned with another part of the dream, that which offers as the purpose of life something more than survival: the search for truth and the pursuit of happiness.

The presence of these two classes of institution—the pragmatic and the ideal—reflects a dichotomy which may be seen in all societies, but it is more critical in our own. Historically, American culture has prized two contradictory sets of values: self-reliance and initiative on the one hand, cooperative goals on the other. The assumption that material success brings spiritual rewards has exacerbated the ambiguity of the American dream. As a result, we wish to accomplish political ends but also wish to be loved for doing so; we are impelled to act in one way, but to offer justification for our action in another. We have a tendency to apply contradictory sets of standards to our behavior, and we often suffer as a result. It would be useful to consider that instead of continuing to see the dichotomy as inevitable, we should think of it as a set of complementary values, going hand in hand.

UNIVERSITIES AS SPECIAL BODIES

Universities are not essentially pragmatic institutions. They are devoted to the pursuit and transmission of knowledge, and they are founded upon the conviction that what they do has moral rather than expedient value. They are thus measurable by their ideals rather than by the immediate effect of what they do. Their special position is well recognized in society: universities are freely and generously supported by tax moneys and in many States given constitutional autonomy. They are not fashioned to produce profit in monetary terms: they are meant to count their profit in the enrichment of life and in the preservation of ideals.

Given this special character of universities, it seems only natural to conclude that they are outside society, exempt from the need to provide for the general as well as the special welfare. The professor often draws up his gown whenever he sees a danger that practical mud might splatter it: he often sees himself as isolated in a tower, insulated from street noise, helpless in affairs of the world. Such a conclusion is false, and it is misinformed to think that universities can, or should, operate outside society. Moreover, once we recognize that Government is the *fons et caput* of social organization, we must also recognize that it is proper for Government to draw upon the resources of other institutions in society—including the universities.

THE RESPONSIBILITIES OF UNIVERSITIES

Thus, it is misguided to argue that universities should remain aloof and should never enter the marketplace or the legislative halls. It is misguided, in the name of "purity," to suggest that universities should withhold from society the contributions they are uniquely fitted to make.

First of all, this kind of isolation is in any case impossible. Universities are composed of men and women who have lives in society—who are as political, economic, and active as anybody else. The bell which tolls for society tolls as loudly for them, and they may not renounce this basic responsibility for the character of their times. Second, universities exist in, and reflect their societies; and they cannot disentangle themselves from the social fabric in which they exist. The special place which universities have in society does not imply separation; it implies freedom from any restriction on their ability to carry out their special function. This is more than a

85

theoretical demand. Without this freedom, universities cannot survive.

UNIVERSITIES AND GOVERNMENT

As a special body, therefore, the university must have a special relationship to government; one which reflects its idiosyncratic features but which does not isolate it. The university cannot and should not engage in any governmental activity which will compromise, modify, or destroy its special functions. As a corollary, however, it must and should engage in governmental activities which do none of these. Freedom has the other face of responsibility; unwillingness to accept one will surely destroy the other. Neither a university, nor any institution, nor any individual can have it both ways.

It is therefore proper for Government to make use of university resources in the pursuit of national aims; but it must understand, when it does so, that it is not merely adding another governmental organization to its existing structures. It has certainly been pleasing to the Government to find in universities the tables of organization and cadres which the Army admires, and to see in them the answer to urgent needs. It is convenient to draw upon organized concentrations of experts, and no government can be blamed which delights in this.

This governmental delight, however, has been matched by squeals of joy in the academy. The motives are varied, but among them can be noted the fact that Government service provides a prestige which campuses do not; that the professor may get the feeling which universities tend to depress, that he is in the center of things; that the slow ascent of an upward mobile may be accelerated into exhilarating flight. If the Government tends to use the professor, the professor is often deferential, glad to be of use, willing to swell a scene or two. And so are the universities—for profit, for prestige, for the opportunities to orbit deans around the world.[20] They should not be blamed; a little bit of this is in all of us.

THE INHERENT DANGERS

Comprendre, say the French, *c'est tout pardonner*. This may not be applicable in this instance, for the consequences of thoughtless and uncontrolled governmental use of universities are serious —for Government, for universities, and hence for the society of which they are important parts.

[20] See, e.g., Walter Adams and John A. Garraty, "Is the World Our Campus?" East Lansing: Michigan State University Press, 1960.

If universities are put to governmental use in an unlimited fashion, there can only result a tragic diminution of their special functions, which will no longer be carried out. When universities become merely an arm of Government, they begin to dispense conventional orthodoxy instead of pursuing free inquiry; to serve as advocates rather than analysts; to accept ritualistic answers instead of grappling with difficult questions; above all, to abandon their necessary and natural function as counterweights to the pragmatic evaluation normal in Government. When this happens, their occupation, like Othello's, disappears, and the whole society is impoverished. Then, Government becomes monolithic, expedient, motivated only by its own empirical momentum. And, society's pluralistic fabric is irreparably damaged.

An extreme example is the degradation of the Nazi state and the willingness of the German universities to give moral and intellectual color to the pragmatic programs of the leaders: they clothed apes in doctoral gowns and blessed them with their diplomas. By converting themselves from homes for philosophical diversity into propaganda centers for an official doctrine,[21] they legitimized a totalitarian, monolithic regime and drained the moral and intellectual lifeblood from the German nation. And, after defeat, this depleted society was almost totally devoid of the leaders who could help rebuild a moral order. The example is extreme, but the lesson is clear: the collapse of universities can mean the collapse of a whole society, and since Government governs a whole society, it loses in the long run when it forces roles and functions to become blurred.

Neither expediency nor pragmatism implies, however, the absence of morality. It is a question of degree and emphasis. Universities can function most usefully by devoting themselves exclusively to their proper domains. In doing so, though, they may quite properly be helpful in other areas. What is required more than anything else is an honesty of purpose and an honesty of aim, on the part of Government and the universities together.

THE DEEPER DIMENSION OF THE CREDIBILITY GAP

In recent years, under the many pressures of modern society, we have witnessed a persistent degradation of values through their

21 Robert Hutchins underscores the basic incompatibility between free universities and "homogeneous" societies: "Educational systems and universities in countries that have militant official philosophies may be able to cope with industrialization and specialization. . . . But they cannot cope with philosophical diversity. They cannot allow it. They have to take the view that the last word has been said, or at least the last important word, and that to permit the addition of another is to promote error and endanger the unity and safety of the state." Op. cit., p. 67.

use for ulterior and expedient ends. The cynical use of values from one system to justify the purposes of another system can only result in the ultimate destruction of the values themselves, which cease to move men, and which are no longer capable of acting as guides to conduct. More important, this misuse causes a fundamental credibility gap.

The term "credibility gap" is most often used to express the distinction between what is said and what is true: it rests on the circumstance that when, in a given situation, false or partial information is imparted, the conclusions cannot be believed. The cure for this, of course, may rightly be sought in the full disclosure of truth, and while this may not always be easy to accomplish, it is nonetheless a sovereign remedy at hand. With respect to the expedient use of values, however, the meaning of "credibility" changes. Instead of being related to the distance between truth and falsehood, it reflects a dishonesty of another kind, that which is an inevitable concomitant of any justification by moral principle of a program whose ends are only pragmatic and direct. It is no longer a matter of "truth," but of attitude.

The implication is not, certainly, that expedient ends are wrong or undesirable. It is rather that expedient ends should be justified in terms of themselves, not in terms of larger, universal principles. The elimination of disease, for example, may be justified in terms of moral good; it may also have the practical effect of producing a more efficient soldiery. If the purpose of the Government is to produce the efficient soldiery, that purpose should not be concealed under the alleged humanitarian aim; when this happens, the ostensible reason is seen as false and the Government runs the risk of being considered hypocritical.

Unfortunately we have sometimes missed this point in designing our assistance programs. Often, we have come to be accused of substituting cant for candor; and, to our loss, *timeo Americanos et dona ferentes* has become a pervasive slogan. Yet, failing to recognize the essence of the problem, we have frequently ascribed the weakness of some programs to the garb in which they were clothed, and have then changed the packaging rather than the product.

THE ULTERIOR CAN BE OSTENSIBLE

We may take note that other nations, such as France, equally concerned with their national interests, can pursue them without adverse criticism and without adverse results. They project, although they do the same things, a different image.

The French have for many years, and openly, subsidized educational and economic programs all over the world. They have never denied that they have expected benefits to accrue to France: in the words of M. Jean Basdevant, Director General of Cultural and Technical Affairs at the French Ministry of Foreign Affairs, "France intends to encourage the spread of the French language, that incomparable means of expression" and to assist in the "training of a foreign intelligentsia and cadres," and in the "spread of French culture in all its forms." [22] Two aspects of this program deserve special attention: (1) France expects to advance its national interests and to maintain a certain dominion; (2) France believes that the inherent values of its own language and civilization, without distortion, are such as to attract the permanent admiration of all who come in contact with them.

As a result, French overseas programs are within themselves beyond reproach: their educational standards are equal to those at home in curriculum and staff; those who engage in them are integrated into the regular French educational organizations and are not put into the subsidiary categories which our overseas professors often occupy. The difference between the French experience and our own lies in attitude. Where the French believe in the values they proclaim, we are ambivalent toward our own.

The ambivalence is not that of Government servants too often made into whipping boys: it is the fundamental ambivalence of our society.[23] Since we see books at home as "useful," we see them in that light abroad; since we think at home in terms of images, we select our overseas materials accordingly. The holdings of the average American library abroad are not only small; they are, to put it bluntly, dull. Moreover, they reflect the basis of choice, showing not America as it is, but America as we would like it to appear. Since in our value system the concrete is more important than the abstract, we devote scant appropriations to books, heavy appropriations to tangible aids. Ideas, seen in many segments of our culture as objects to be manipulated, are exported, along with their professorial vehicles, as so many items. The typical bill of lading, says the cynic, contains one scholar, one set of texts, one trunk, one idea on

[22] "France's Cultural Action Throughout The World," New York: Ambassade de France, Service de Presse et d'Information, August 1965.

[23] Homer Babbidge, president of the University of Connecticut, points out that our goals in international affairs are "too consciously sought" and that we are "too narrowly concerned with demonstrable results, and hence with utilitarian programs." He thinks "we have to come to grips with the issue of whether or not our goal is true international understanding—weaknesses and all—or a kind of cultural one-upmanship. There is," he says, "a conflict here between our expressed desire to promote understanding, and our understandable but nonetheless regrettable preoccupation with good-impressionism." "Peace, Understanding, and Education," reprinted in "Brademas Compendium," pp. 59, 60.

89

the value of democracy, one insight, and two dependents. The ulterior becomes ostensible when we begin to believe in what we say we believe.

THE PRAGMATIC ARGUMENT AGAINST CYNICISM

What American universities and professors accomplish abroad, for the interests of their country, is not a specific task, but a general one of reflecting the values of the United States in their persons, their actions, and their attitudes. With due respect to other nations, these values are not inconsiderable; we have much to be proud of. Indeed, we are better than we permit ourselves to seem. When a professor, as an individual or as a member of a university team, is subsidized to accomplish a specific political goal, he not only fails, but traduces his real role at home and abroad. The recent involvement of a major university with the Ngo Dinh Diem government of Viet-Nam is sadly to the point. Foreign policy belongs to Government, not to universities; it belongs to officers of the State Department, not to departments of political science. A blurring of these distinctions results in a double failure: the professor fails as professor, and he fails as diplomat as well. The Nation gains virtually nothing.

Cynicism thus means failure. Success requires, at a minimum, an abiding belief by Government and the universities in what each is doing. University programs must therefore be impeccable in themselves, and not subject to modification to fit expedient ends. University programs cannot be used to implement transient policies unless these transient policies are in accord with their primary aims of advancing knowledge and alleviating distress.[24] The pressures on the Government, being largely pragmatic, may cause it to approach universities pragmatically. Government should not be criticized for trying, but it should not always be encouraged to succeed. The officer of the Government and the university administrator must each judge his activities in terms of his primary adhesion to organizational goals; if he does not, he is ineffective. In short, the two roles, and the two functions, must be kept apart, which is not to

[24] Charles Frankel, professor of philosophy at Columbia University, and currently Assistant Secretary of State for Educational and Cultural Affairs, emphasizes that "information" and "propaganda" on the one side and "education" and "culture" on the other each have distinct objectives which should not be mixed. He points out that "an information program tends to embarrass and compromise an educational and cultural program when it is too closely and visibly associated with it. For the central commitment of an information program is quite properly to the U.S. foreign policy of the moment, accepted as given, while the commitment of an educational and cultural program is to open-ended inquiry, the free exchange of opinions, and the search for a common ground for mutual understanding." "The Neglected Aspect of Foreign Affairs," Washington: The Brookings Institution, 1966, p. 33.

say that there can be no complementary area where both can work in harmony without loss. After all, wherever he works, every citizen is part of American society. He will contribute best to its welfare by doing his own job as well as he can, with respect for what others are doing. And, what is true for Americans as individuals is equally true for American institutions.

THE SUM OF THE ARGUMENTS

It is to the advantage of both Government and the universities that the distinction between their activities be kept clear. The society which no longer has an autonomous university function within it has lost its pluralist strength, and is therefore a poorer society. Universities, however, cannot function without the pragmatic activities of Government, so that, in effect, each needs the other, and each profits from the other. Attempts to make universities into arms of political policy blur this distinction and thus weaken the entire society.

In addition, however, such attempts have also been pragmatic failures. We stand today at a curious point where morality and expediency, often mutually exclusive, in fact go hand in hand. If there is no excuse, from a moral point of view, for an immoral program, there is even less excuse for an immoral program which does not work. Motive is less important than the actions it brings about: even for those who have no wish to be pure in principle it is sensible to be pure as a matter of practicality. The interests of the intellectual community and those of the Government in fact coincide: by hewing to an honest line, both hew to an effective one. Honesty is good; but in addition, honesty pays. In short, it is possible to have the best of both possible worlds.

THE PRESCRIPTION
GOVERNMENTAL COMMITMENT TO
INTERNATIONAL EDUCATION

In recent years our traditional commitment to the ideals of education has been enlarged by an international dimension. President Johnson articulated the new commitment eloquently and persuasively—first in his Smithsonian address of 1965 and later in his special message to Congress on February 2, 1966:

Education lies at the heart of every nation's hopes and purposes. It must be at the heart of our international relations. . . . International education cannot be the work of one country. It is the responsibility and promise of all nations. It calls for free exchange and full collaboration. We

91

expect to receive as much as we give, to learn as well as to teach. Let this Nation play its part.

The congressional response to this challenge was prompt and unmistakable. The International Education Act of 1966 endorsed the commitment, and provided the framework for implementing it. But it was only the first step. It left a crucial question unanswered: whether we would tolerate, as in international education efforts of the past, a glaring gap between the expression of ideals and their realization—a gap sometimes so large as to impeach, in skeptical minds, the sincerity of the commitment itself.

Clearly, it is time to make reality conform to ideal, to allow "conduct to be an unspoken sermon," and to make practice congruent with precept. The manner in which a nation allocates its scarce resources, the manner in which it spends its public treasure, is the most revealing index of its values and priorities—the clearest reflection of the relative importance it attaches to the things in which it believes. If we mean what we say, therefore, if we adhere to the values enunciated by President Johnson, we must translate that conviction into the unambiguous dollar terms of governmental budgets. We must provide significant, massive, and comprehensive financial support for international education in its broadest sense; and this means support for American higher education on a scale unparalleled in history.

Some profess that universities cannot maintain their autonomy unless they have nothing to do with governmental activities. This is erroneous. In fact, universities' independence is greater when funds are available which enable them adequately to carry out their tasks, and few universities today have the requisite private resources to do so.

CAPITAL AND SUSTAINING GRANTS

In order to strengthen the universities for a role in international education, the Government should change the character and shift the emphasis of its financial support from mission-oriented project grants to sustaining capital grants. It should provide stable, long-range, continuing, and predictable funding for research and instructional programs in international education, so as to build up the universities' fundamental academic capabilities for discharging their international responsibilities. It should make an investment in the universities rather than merely buying services from them.

The idea of capital grants is by no means revolutionary. The Government has already made modest gestures in this direction with the new institutional grants of the National Science Foundation, the general research support and facilities grants to medical schools by the National Institutes of Health, the sustaining university grants of the National Aeronautics and Space Administration, and the Office of Education grants to universities for buildings and equipment. The model exists; it remains to be elaborated, generalized, and systematized.

Unlike the "overhead" support from mission-oriented projects, a system of institutional capital grants provides "an economic and feasible way of enlarging the international competence of higher education in the United States" and gives "society at large a much greater reserve strength for its international commitments in the long run." [25] Such support is aimed at the central nervous system of the universities—the academic and the scholarly. Such support does not require that universities change their roles or their belief systems, nor that the universities transform their character in order to qualify. Such support inhibits the growth on campuses of administrative units which merely ape their governmental counterparts. Such support slows the proliferation of administrative sheep in academic garb, and discourages the appearance of academic floorwalkers who pace the peripheries of the university world without knowledge or interest or concern. Instead, such support contributes to the growth and enrichment of intellectual disciplines, which have inherent validity as well as potential usefulness, such as international politics and diplomacy; comparative government and economic systems; population and public health; international trade and economic development; languages and linguistics; human development, education, and child development.

It is this kind of support which the Congress envisioned, with commendable breadth of understanding and principle, in the International Education Act of 1966; it is the kind of support which will make it possible for universities to be the places they should be —where it is possible, in the words of William Nagle, "to dream, to think, to act as intellectual gadflies in our society, to question. . . ."[26] Such support will make the university commentator and critic, thinker and innovator, that can engage Government in that kind of dialog which brings about progress.

The country deserves no less. Whatever formula is finally adopted for allocating capital grants among the universities,[27] this

[25] Miller, op. cit., pp. 69–70.
[26] Nagle, op. cit., p. 317.
[27] One possibility is the formula proposed in the Miller bill (H.R. 875, 90th Cong.). Another alternative is to tie the capital grants to the size of an institution's research budget, the number of undergraduates it trains, and the number of advanced degrees it grants over a five-year base period. Some allowance, of course, would have to be made for "smaller" institutions and for "newcomers" to the field of international education.

basic investment in education is far better in principle than the use of stylized contractual programs designed to accomplish specific, short-term aims and containing within them the seeds of serious liabilities. It is also far superior in practice.

CAPITAL GRANTS AND THE COVETOUSNESS OF UNIVERSITIES

The belief is not uncommon that in Government-university relationships it is the university which has been corrupted by deliberate and seductive blandishment. Such a belief is only partly true, and overlooks the fact that few seductions are successful where there has not been a similarity of values. A bait is refused which is not considered delicious. Certainly Government has attempted to make participation in its programs attractive to the universities, but it found a most ready willingness on their part. In some cases not much was required: the offer of access to an Embassy soda fountain has lured many a scholar from his lore; the vision of an expanded jurisdiction has entranced a score of deans. The fact is that universities have coveted what the Government has offered, and so long as they continue to see profit—in funds, buildings, enlargement or prestige—in Government programs, they will continue to covet them. The system of capital investments reduces this covetousness to normal proportions and channels it into constructive lines: where the major profit will be in terms of fundamental academic values, there can be no objection to a desire to have it.

It would be naïve to suppose, however, that the capital grants we have proposed will eliminate completely the system of mission-oriented project contracts. This means that a mechanism must be developed which will provide the necessary safeguards against potential abuse. Criteria must be spelled out to guide government and the universities in their contract relationship. External checks must be established, on both Government and the universities, to achieve two basic objectives: the diminution of academic covetousness on the one hand, and the desire of Government for a precipitate satisfaction of immediate and transitory needs, on the other. Only through a selective application of these checks can a climate be created in which project contracts make a useful contribution—without compromising the Government-university relationship.

WHAT THE GOVERNMENT MUST DO

1. Every project suggested for implementation by a university should, in the first instance, be submitted to a professional panel drawn from national associations such as the American Economic

Association, the Modern Language Association, the American Hospital Association, and the like.[28]

2. Each such project should be examined by the panel in order to determine:

(a) whether the project is inherently valid in terms of professional criteria;

(b) whether the project, even though professionally valid, is suitable for a university to undertake; and

(c) which universities have the requisite resources in faculty and facilities to assure the probable success of the project.

3. Any project deemed unsuitable by the panel, for any of the above reasons, will be abandoned by the Government insofar as implementation by universities is concerned.

4. Any acceptable project will be offered by Government to the universities suggested by the panel in order of their competence for that project. Under these conditions the Government will know that it is approaching the "right" university; the university will have reasonable assurance that the project is professionally sound, and that its involvement will be free from reproach, taint, or ambiguity.

5. The Government will reimburse the university only for direct costs. There will be no overhead.

WHAT THE UNIVERSITIES MUST DO

The absence of overhead funds will, of course, have been offset by the extensive capital grants from Government which we have proposed. The "no overhead" rule, however, will produce another desirable result: it will weaken the university's temptation to apply other than academic standards to projects suggested by the Government. To put it unambiguously, the profit will have been taken out of the contract system, and the munificent fringe benefits will no longer be operative as attractive inducements. The university will then do what it must do:

1. Consider each project in the light of its own intellectual standards and capabilities.

2. Compute the cost of the project in terms of the diver-

[28] The rationale of this suggestion rests on the belief that the professions are an important safeguard against organizational bureaucracies, in and out of government. As John W. Gardner points out, "The loyalty of the professional man is to his profession and not to the organization that may house him at any given moment. . . . The men the chemist thinks of as his colleagues are not those who occupy neighboring offices, but his fellow professionals wherever they may be throughout the country, even throughout the world." "Self-Renewal," New York: Harper & Row, 1964, p. 83.

sion of staff and resources from its on-campus teaching and research functions.

3. Evaluate the project in terms of its internal value system, its intellectual priorities, and its multiple responsibilities.

4. Estimate the long-range contribution that the project is likely to make to the strengthening of the university as an educational institution.

5. Reappraise the value to the university of the contract promoters and project salesmen—and encourage these now-redundant mountebanks to seek more compatible climates.

In short, the absence of overhead will compel the universities to make their "cost-benefit" analysis of proposed projects in real terms rather than money terms.

THE PROGNOSIS

GENERAL EFFECTS

This suggested prescription may be defended in terms of principle; it may also be defended as practical. Universities would be the great beneficiaries of such a change in policy, for in return for giving up the obvious and immediate advantages of overhead support, they would lay rightful claim to a support far more meaningful: financial backing for their real work in the form of general, capital investment grants by Government. By putting this money to use in the strengthening of the established disciplines and in the encouragement of new and imaginative fields of inquiry, the universities would reap genuine, not spurious, renown. By expanding intellectually rather than in the size of empire, the universities would divest themselves of unattractive personnel and come closer to a realization of their identity. The graduates of such universities would be better equipped to serve their country, in or out of Government. The universities would retain their autonomy and yet recognize their responsibilities to society. American pluralism would be reinforced—to the general benefit of all sectors of society, pragmatic and theoretical. And, in a world tending so greatly to fall under the sway of monolithic governments, a pluralistic America, with free dialog, and proper separation of functions, would stand as an important and powerful example.

SPECIFIC EFFECTS

In the course of time, the number and scope of contract programs would tend to diminish, and those which remained would be carefully selected. A certain number of programs, especially those unsuitable for universities, but necessary for Government, would have to be undertaken either by private or by governmental organizations; in any case, by appropriate organizations. The Government would receive full value from universities and not be short-changed, through the circumstance of "buying" from them only that which they are fitted to "sell." The links between the professions and the Government would be strengthened, with a corresponding increase in understanding of the different standards and values. Graduates of universities would be better equipped to serve and our overseas programs would be increasingly free from the dichotomy which we have mentioned. A period of administrative readjustment would ensue, but along with it would come a reassessment and a reaffirmation of values, a clarification of identity, an openness of purpose, and an end to the ambiguity which has only served to create misunderstanding and to obscure the fact that most men, if given the chance to know and to appreciate who they are, are men of good will. A democracy can ask for no more to achieve success.

Commentary
Review of the Adams-Jaffe Paper

Jacob Canter

Walter Adams and Adrian Jaffe have done a masterful job. Not only have they diagnosed vividly, analytically, and imaginatively the current crisis in identity facing our universities; they have also prescribed. During my first reading of their paper, I found much with which I, and probably any of us, would freely associate: the fear (real or imagined) of coercion, seduction, and control of scholarship and scholars by government; the concern over the possibility, if not the incidence, of "short changing" the government; the challenging, provocative postulates regarding academic ethics and sponsored research; the persistent conflict between the idealistic and pragmatic systems of values as applied to university-government relationships.

These, and the other diagnostic questions raised in the paper, I felt, reflect not only the *malaise* of the universities toward themselves and toward their relationships with government; they implied and sometimes made explicit a great, perhaps greater, dilemma of our times. That is, the disparate and frequently ambiguous roles played by our institutions *vis-a-vis* their students, their societies, and the world community of scholars and intellectuals. In evidence are the symptoms: the "sale" of intellectual products; the appearance of "marginal personnel"; the quest for federal contracts to perform services and projects separated from the central and traditional purposes of the university.

My first reading of the paper also led me to agree with the Adams-Jaffe prescription both in general and specific terms, though I might disagree with some of the dosages recommended. I certainly agree with the need for large support for international education. The dimensions of our international educational needs dictate therapeutic treatment of our entire educational system with unprecedented thoroughness.

And I would personally buy a package that included long-term capital grants to universities by government, *along with* the purchase of specific services.

For I do not believe that government is yet in a position to dispense with grants for specific services or for research and analysis. These will continue to be needed for some time. There are wide areas of critical needs in research and development that universities not only *appropriately* supply; frequently the universities are the *only* source of supply.

I also wonder about the desirability of further layering through the creation of professional review panels that the paper recommends.

It was at this point of departure from a hitherto acceptable thesis that I turned back and reread the provocative arguments which prefaced the general thesis. The need for professional review panels appeared to be predicated upon not only the justified claim of greater expertise but also upon a shared academic *belief system.*

In all candor, I found myself reviewing with the authors the sociopsychological basis for the crisis in identity. I found myself reviewing their interpretation of the history and development of the American educational belief system.

While Jefferson in the eighteenth century, and Eliot in the nineteenth, did recognize that education must serve the community in practical ways, both the community and the practical ways were narrowly confined. There was much in their belief system that few in this room would find tolerable today.

For example, both, as we know, deplored the reckless practice of sending students abroad for education. Jefferson felt that an American who goes to Europe for his education "loses in his knowledge, in his morals, in his habits, and in his happiness." Eliot, afraid that American students abroad might become "citizens of the world," once flatly stated that cosmopolitans "are, as a rule, an unhappy, useless, and sterile breed."

We, today, with our announced and virtually unanimous support for international education, could hardly accept any traditional academic belief system which contained these postulates.

In short, in my comment, I am led to question the underpinnings of a *traditional* definition of academic purpose, given this narrow focus of its base. Is it not possible that traditional parochialism in our education is central to the university's difficulty in relating to an expanded, worldwide, social environment?

If we are indeed to discuss higher education in the public international service, I believe we must first ask whether our traditional belief system, our equipment and resources, our knowledge of the world community (scholarly or otherwise), and our governmental apparatus are relevant to the larger world to which we seek to—in fact, must—relate. It could be that we are quite unprepared.

I believe that we must ask other questions too. First, is the sole or even the primary role of the American university today one of instructing our students? Does the accumulation of other, even subsidiary, functions necessarily produce such ambiguity as to endanger the integrity and the future functioning of education?

Secondly, has the educational community in the United States codified a contemporary belief system relevant to the world today? Does it, or should it, include a modicum of responsibility toward shared experiences, shared vocabulary, and shared knowledge with scholars from abroad? Has the world of scholarship, using the tools of scholarship, taken inventories of its basic world needs?

Thirdly, have we, as Americans, consciously considered the role of the intellectual and his relation to his own society? Have our intellectuals really developed a thesis regarding their relevance to society, their participation in, or—if they prefer—alienation from government and governmental activities at any level?

Finally, do participation and the acceptance of broader responsibilities really conflict with the integrity, autonomy and pluralistic strength of the university as an institution and of the scholar-intellectual as an individual?

In all of these questions, whatever the answers, whatever the choices, have we examined them? have we made the choices? have we checked the validity of all the assumptions? and have we seriously prepared for the future, even knowing what it meant, as Don Price put it in the famous limerick? That limerick, by the way, presupposes, of course, that all the men who wined and dined the Lady from Kent were of single mind and purpose.

Which may be true. But it may not.

Commentary
Remarks of
Professors Adams and Jaffe

The authors made several comments to summarize their paper and open the discussions of it: We have no objection at all to full university participation in suitable governmental affairs. We start out suggesting there has come to be a confusion of roles between two qualitatively different kinds of institutions, the government, a pragmatic kind of institution, and the university which judges its program in relation to certain kinds of ideals it holds. We use neither term in a pejorative way, only as a means to distinguish the ways by which these two kinds of institutions must attest to the effectiveness of their actions. Government must decide in terms of what is most effective in achieving its policies. Universities must judge the programs in which they participate in relation to certain ideals they hold.

We then suggest that the pluralism of the United States requires the co-existence of several different kinds of institutions, and further that the presence of a pragmatic institution and an idealistic institution are of equal importance to society. The pluralism of the society suffers if these distinctions between different kinds of institutions become blurred. There is particular reason to maintain the particular autonomies of both the government and the universities, a retention of autonomy which does not preclude the necessary and important interdependence of the two. It is a matter of keeping the two separate roles separated to avoid the unfortunate consequences that result from confusing them, not the least of which is the shortchanging of the government. When the government calls upon a university for a particular project, it has a right to get the kind of service the university is peculiarly able to provide, that is, objective analysis of a situation of an order which one cannot expect in other segments of society in quite the same way. If it is getting services analogous to those which agencies within the government can provide, it is not getting what it is entitled to from the university in the way of opinion and advice.

Compiled by
Elizabeth N.
Shiver

101

The second important confusion over roles is one which leads to an insiduous erosion of the university program itself. Regardless of the nature of the work, if the university is acting as an analogue of government, those matters of educational importance on campus tend to become eroded and ultimately to disappear. In allocation of time, resources, and interests, the educational interests that are peculiarly the universities' are likely to be left out of the consideration in the pressure of analogous behavior. A third unfortunate result of this confusion is the growth on campus of what we consider peripheral academic personnel filling a very particular kind of nonacademic role.

We speak also of the problem of a credibility gap, that is, the gap between the pragmatic ends of any given program, and the moral justification given for it. Institutions offer so-called moral justification for programs which have only pragmatic and expedient ends. There is a necessity for society and for the universities in particular to believe in the values they proclaim. There is a gap between what we say we believe and what we actually believe, and a great deal of pious cant is heard about the importance of ideas, of books, or culture, and all the other academic values when in fact these values are frequently not held at all. The values are really a series of manipulated images. And, with the universities and the government equally to blame, we have come to look in this country on ideas, on moral values, on books, and on attitudes as one more commodity to be manipulated, one more image to be sent out into the world and not as things that have their own inherent value. We make a contrast between our own experience here and that of some other countries. We do not object to the intelligent use of educational materials for whatever effect they may have to our national advantage in foreign countries. We have seen no diffidence on the part of other countries in promoting their own literature, culture, and art with the distinction however that they admit what they are doing. They are not ashamed of this type of activity, nor unwilling to admit that some political advantage may accrue as a secondary and ancilliary result of this export.

We say also that it is not unusual for the government to offer universities the kind of support it does offer, but there is not necessarily any good reason why the university should be quite so willing to accept everything offered, and indeed to come seeking what it may have missed. The universities have failed to look at government programs in the light of how appropriate they are for the university. We do not think anyone is to blame, or that the situation is surprising, but in looking to the future and the danger of both the universities and government losing autonomy, we thought one thing that could be done is to take some of the temptation away and make it easier for those who claim intellectual values to demonstrate them. And this is one reason we suggest as a corollary to our capital grants proposal that the whole business of contract proposals should finally come to an end, because we feel that inherent in any such relationship there are dangers of such an order that we would all be better off perhaps if we would minimize them insofar as possible.

Essentially, we are making three points. First, the contract system as practiced in the past has not worked too well in terms of the national goals we have set. Second, the major reason for this failure is the blurring of roles between the government and the universities. The resulting crisis of identity we contend has shortchanged both partners in this relationship. Third, the proposal for reform is to change the pay-off matrix to induce the type of behavior which will yield the desired results. The basic idea is to suggest a major shift in emphasis from the project, mission-oriented contract to a system of capital or sustaining grants; and beyond that point, if any project grants are to be made, the profit should be taken out of them in the form of the overhead allowance. Remove the temptation which the overhead allowance symbolizes. The system of capital grants would give the university the underlying basic academic support which it needs in order to discharge its functions both internally and as a servant of the larger society. Another part of our proposal is that each project should pass an additional screening safeguard through submission to a professional panel before being submitted to a university. The panel would try to decide whether the project was inherently valid in terms of professional criteria and second, whether the project was suitable for the university to undertake even if it is professionally valid, and finally, which universities have the requisite resources in faculty and facilities to assure the probable success of the project.

We do not mean to suggest that all projects will come to an end or that mission-oriented activity would not go on. It is a question of how much and what kind. We feel that many of the projects which universities have undertaken did not germinate from the university's interest but had their origins outside. We object to the university and people within the university being contract seekers rather than contract takers on the grounds that this approach shortchanges the government and the university. In this situation the government is not really in contact with the core of the university. It is not deriving the academic benefit which the

103

university has to offer. If the university is truly service oriented, it will undertake only those projects that have inherent academic value and at the same time provide a service to the community. The conflict here, or the dichotomy, is not as great as one might suppose. It is the terms of reference which are used to draw up the project, the terms of cooperation between government and the university which need to be ironed out and which we think can be ironed out.

Commentary
Summary of
the Discussion*

The Seminar discussion revealed substantial disagreement with the crisis of identity thesis and with the recommendations advanced to resolve this crisis and to resolve the problems of government-academic relationships. There was some agreement in principle with the concept of grants to educational institutions and the need for general sustaining support to strengthen institutions. It was acknowledged that there have been many problems in existing systems of governmental support to institutions, and that the essential idea of moving heavily to institutional grants would be one factor tending to minimize somewhat certain of the understandable and legitimate pressures which collectively have led to undesirable results for the university.

Elizabeth N. Shiver

In addition, the categorical support of contracts had led too many university administrators and faculty to move from the wrong end of the spectrum, to seek the sources of funds, then build their programs accordingly. This has tended to distort the university's programs, to overbalance them in one way or another. The superior flexibility of sustaining grants would provide the support the institution needs to carry on its basic and central program, support that does not produce imbalance. Imbalance frequently results from the innovative and glamorous activities that attract support, activities the institution may be undertaking because the support is available. These activities can make the operation of the institution more difficult in the long run. Rather than support for innovation, support is needed for activities essential to the operation of an institution, such as salaries for professors teaching basic courses, operation of the physical plant, operation of the library. Basic support to strengthen international activities and programs is very

* Several of the propositions and proposals in the paper by Professors Adams and Jaffe provoked spirited discussion during the Seminar and gave rise as well to a number of communications from participants and others who had read the paper, including the Committee on Governmental Relations of the National Association of College and University Business Officers. In preparing the summary, account has been taken of these communications as well as the Seminar discussions.

much needed as evidenced by the overwhelming endorsement by the academic community of the International Education Act of 1966 which would provide some support of this kind.

Nonetheless, sustaining grants were seen as an ill-suited mechanism for mission-oriented projects or for meeting any of the government's needs for specific services. The contention was that grants could not successfully replace contracts but that the university could use both means of funding for different purposes. Further, the negative argument put forth supporting the grant concept on grounds that contract overhead allowances constitute an opportunity to make financial profit was viewed as highly questionable if not spurious.

Seminar reaction was mixed regarding the possibility that contracts and categorical support in general basically have "distorted" university programs and objectives. Those who did not seriously credit the possibility pointed out that many institutions have made a scrupulous selection of projects and have kept their overseas activities in a manageable form, even to the extent that the most utilitarian of undertakings have yielded an important contribution to the academic program. Those who accepted distortion as a possibility appeared to believe that, at least in their own institutions, it was kept to a minimal and manageable level.

There were objections raised to the picture drawn of the professor overseas, and to the entire notion that he is diminishing his obligations to his students by working overseas. In several fields the world is quite literally the professor's laboratory, and he should go out into it, and furthermore, he should take his students with him. Additional reaction was that neither the professor nor the educational institution as a whole can be realistically viewed as overcommitted in international programs. To the contrary, there is not enough involvement in international affairs, not enough institutional interest in or recognition of the importance of this aspect of the educational enterprise.

Strong objections were also raised to what was called a completely false dichotomy between the pragmatic and idealistic institutions. The idea that an institution cannot be practical and idealistic at the same time was rejected by those who found the argument comparable to the debate over pure and applied research. There should be no denial of idealism in assuming responsibility for solving a practical problem. It is the same as insisting that pure research is no longer pure if it eventually has a practical application. There are institutions and individuals within institutions who clearly see the connection between theoretical and scholarly endeavor and practical application to the problems of the world.

There is a suggestion in the authors' rationale that all institutions are following one pattern, but there are other patterns in this country, successful patterns of combining scholarly endeavor and service in the best sense of the word.

Regardless of the appeal of the grant concept and the agreement that grants would provide badly needed support, the Seminar stressed the need to be realistic in considering the problems involved in long-term, sustaining support from the government for international education. It also warned against the idea that capital grants would offer a permanent resolution of several complex relationships. It is well to understand initially that the concept of institutional grants will not serve as a cure-all for the problems of government—academic relationships, nor will it cure any crisis of identity. There are as many dangers and problems inherent in the grant proposal as there are in the various kinds of categorical support now in effect. Insofar as grants are seen as an escape from categories, they will simply necessitate the use of larger categories or different categories. In addition, there are several broad categories other than the international one for which grants would be wanted. The proposed grant system would do very little to solve the basic problems in the international area.

Insofar as grants are viewed as an escape from projects and contracts, there is a failure to consider the continuing governmental need for specific services. Not only are questions of governmental need for specific services left unanswered, but also the equally hard questions of public accountability and the provision of broad support for developing institutional strength widely in the international area. The government has very real and urgent needs for services it has met through contract support for university activities. It has chosen contract support not only because of Congressional surveillance, but also because there is a direct and obvious connection between the government's needs, or the national interest, and the support the government provides, a *quid pro quo*. If a move is made toward institutional grants, what obligation would the institution carry with long-term support to provide services, both in a general way and in technical assistance specifically? The limitations imposed by grants, or the obligations of the institution, are unclear. The government's need for specific services will continue, and the universities are in many instances the best, and sometimes the only, source of the services that are needed. Though there may be an overlap of interests between the government and the institution, there are also differences; hence, the problem of governmental need cannot be resolved through a system of grants to universities.

107

Indeed, the government may receive a smaller return for its investment.

Recognizing that the contract mechanism is likely to continue, the authors suggested the imposition of a check on the system by professional screening panels. These panels would be responsible for determining the validity of the proposed project, the suitableness of the project for a university operation, and for identifying the institutions capable of undertaking the project. Several objections were raised to this procedure.

In general, it means a further layering of responsibility, an additional complication in moving forward on any given project. The university-government relationship is already burdened with a plethora of review panels, most of which draw heavily on university faculty, consuming a great amount of faculty time, especially the time of senior and experienced scholars. More basic objections than these over inconvenience were raised, however. Surrender by the government of its authority to decide what projects it will undertake and which contractors it will seek is completely unrealistic and improper. Project selection is merely a part of the larger process of policy making and is dependent on decisions about national policy. The final decision on project selection therefore must rest with the government. As for the selection of contractors, the use of professional review panels would tend to concentrate international programs even further in a small number of institutions well known in the international field in direct conflict with the interests of many institutions which want to expand their international activities and in direct conflict with Congressional intent as expressed in the Foreign Assistance Act of 1966. The Foreign Assistance Act authorizes the support of universities through grants to strengthen their competence to engage in technical assistance and developmental activities, to insure that institutions can engage in overseas activities without disrupting ongoing programs. It is a recognition of the responsibility of the government to support those institutions on which it depends for various services to meet governmental needs. It was noted also that professional review panels might serve to inhibit academicians from making proposals for original and creative projects if it were likely that some other institution and some other investigator would be awarded the opportunity to pursue the project.

Quite apart from governmental needs for services, there is the question of public accountability for the use of sustaining grants. Surely, when public funds are spent in support of educational and institutional development, the public is entitled to some defensible accounting of the relationships between the use of funds and the purposes for which the funds were intended. There are appropriate limitations on escaping public accountability. Institutional grants should not be viewed, the Seminar contended, as a means of escaping legitimate and necessary accounting of the use of public funds. Connected with the problem of accountability to Congress there is finally the major problem of the distribution of institutional grants and the purposes to be served. To whom would these grants be distributed and for what purposes? In terms of policies and broad choices, how are guidelines to be established? There is an impression that any and all institutions might be involved although the grant proposal is concerned primarily with grants for overseas activities. Is the proposal actually made in terms of grants for all four-year, degree-granting institutions? What would serve as the mechanism for distributing institutional grants on this scale? It was suggested that the governmental support to the land-grant institutions had been taken as a model without considering that there are less than one hundred institutions in this category. Would the Adams-Jaffe proposal in the end amount only to grants for the larger institutions that are capable of providing the faculty for special projects without dissipating their own programs? If this were the case, the results would be a highly restricted category of institutional grants that could fail to contribute broadly to developing an awareness of international affairs and problems. The development of trained individuals and the development of an informed citizenry that can participate in international and overseas activities is much needed. There are numerous colleges and universities that are in no way prepared to mount overseas operations but which can provide widely distributed strength for developing an informed citizenry and for providing trained individuals for overseas operations. There is confusion here about the institutional grants approach and indeed about the ends and means and purposes to be served. Wrongly applied, this proposal could serve only to increase the unevenness of strength among institutions in international studies and activities.

In addition to the fault the Seminar found in the institutional grants concept as expounded by the authors, there was even sharper disagreement with their reasons for proposing a system of institutional grants. The idea that the grant concept is a prescription for taking the profit motive, the so-called payoff matrix, out of the contract system is based on the faulty premise that overhead allowances on contracts represent a profit. Several of those present believed this allegation to be completely false. Rejected equally strongly was the accusation that universities take government contracts to gain a monetary profit. It is clear that U.S. universities should not be placed in the position of having to subsidize the U.S. government, and this is exactly the situation in which they find themselves if indirect costs are not met on projects undertaken for the government, specifically at the government's request. Universities have contributed of their own resources ever since they began performing an increasing number of tasks for the government which accounts for the struggle they have made over a period of years to have their indirect costs met in a more realistic way. Reimbursement on indirect costs in no way represents a subsidy or a profit but is generally only a partial return for the demands made on university resources. In taking government-supported projects, universities still generally have to contribute their resources; therefore most institutions reject out of hand the notion that they undertake government projects in order to garner a profit which in this sense is implied to be financial.

Institutions certainly do profit or can profit from the governmental activities in which they become involved, but not in a direct financial sense. Any profit which accrues to an institution is in the form of increased capabilities of its faculty in teaching and related activities, increased capabilities that emanate from the overseas service, or other governmentally related service. This kind of profit would be readily acknowledged by those institutions which have had successful experience in government projects, but this in no way represents a direct financial profit. (The Committee on Governmental Relations of the National Association of College and University Business Officers has commented further on the allegation that indirect costs are less valid than direct costs, pointing out that this idea disregards the fact that so-called overhead represents only a return of certain actual costs, determined by the government under Bureau of the Budget regulations, and does not include any element of profit.)

Continuing a wide-ranging discussion on the motivation of the university to undertake government projects, the Seminar considered the factors which induce the university to become involved. The reasons for undertaking government projects vary widely in different situations, but there was strong sentiment among participants that the overriding motivation stems from the professional interests of the faculty and not from any covetousness on the part of the university or its administrators as the authors averred. It is not primarily the availability of funds, nor pressures brought on institutions by the government to accept projects, but rather the pressures of real and genuine professional interests of faculty members which are the strongest forces for involvement. The individual is the initiator, and the man with the ideas and the motivation is the man who will attract the resources to support his work. He feels no lack of dignity in seeking support where the resources are available because he is motivated by his commitment to advance knowledge in his discipline and by his interest in his particular field. As one participant stated, the university administration has been mainly permissive and rather hard put to keep up with the faculty, ever in the hope to stop faculty commitments somewhere short of the university's fiscal capacity.

Recognition that the individual is generally the initiator, the force behind the various activities universities have acquired, was not an attempt on the part of the Seminar to place blame for resulting problems of management upon the scholar. Discussion of these problems led to a strong focus on the uses of a university, the changing role of the university in modern society, and the need for strong administrative leadership in redefining the institution's role. There is the need for a strong institutional definition of its own goals. The institution must recognize its own needs and its goals more clearly if it is to be of service to itself, to the government, or to anyone else. This is the critical point, more so than the method of support, whether this be through contracts, mission-oriented projects, or sustaining grants. Assistant Secretary for Education Paul A. Miller of the Department of Health, Education, and Welfare addressed remarks specifically to this point:

> I do not think the money of the federal government is the evil here. Certainly the programs of the National Science Foundation over the last fifteen years have added greatly to our intellectual resources. My concern is that we have lost, and the faculty perhaps first amongst the leaders of the institution, a kind of integrative planning leading to a distinctive set of aims for the given institution.
>
> Institutions do vary widely in their expectations, in their settings, and in their responsibilities, and in various other ways. I would submit that everyone in American universities has attempted to become an instrumentalist, not the least among them the faculty. We have no one any longer that can be placed in a position to be held accountable for a plan, for a direction. We must rediscover through some kind of procedure a plan to place the university in a position to respond to the multiple obligations it holds. What we have really lost is on the one hand the capability and on the other the courage as administrators and faculty members to deal

with the situation, the pressures, in a strong way; therefore, our institutions have become encrusted with all sorts of special projects. I do not think it is federal support or mission-oriented projects in particular. The real question is: Who is in a position to head the ship and steer it in a definite direction and to be held accountable for it?

It was noted that this kind of problem of leadership and direction is inherent in any specialization of a large bureaucracy. Mention was made several times of the government's similar, though larger, problems of leadership and coordination of its great variety of programs and purposes growing out of diverse legislation and interests. Government is also lacking this highly desirable and perhaps unobtainable clear sense of direction and purpose.

Other comments were added on the likelihood of obtaining the leadership and the wholistic sense of direction for an institution envisioned by Assistant Secretary Miller and others. Can any committee or anybody within the institution really be concerned in a meaningful way with strengthening the entire institution educationally, especially considering the increasing attachment of the individual professor to his discipline or profession rather than to his institution? An alternative suggestion was that a great contribution is being made to meeting problems of external relationships and academic planning by research centers, educational organizations, and learned societies. They are providing leadership and innovative ideas, especially in governmental-academic relationships. They are not serving merely as linkages but as a vital part of the relationship. Nonetheless, it remains the responsibility of the institution to apply the ideas to its particular situation. As for the individual scholar, he is becoming increasingly mobile, increasingly attached to his discipline or profession and less attached to the profession of being a university professor. So long as this trend continues, the distinctions between being attached to an institution and being a part of the government will become less marked, and the growing emphasis on the professional responsibilities of scholars will increase, along with the growing allegiance to the profession. So long as the trend continues, it will serve as a divisive factor within the institution as the institution attempts to move forward with integrative planning for its diverse educational enterprise.

Particularization, specialization, and the expansion of knowledge and scholarship were seen as key factors affecting the institution as it struggles to maintain itself as a cohesive whole. If there is any crisis in identity, any fuzziness in identity, it stems from these factors, not alone from the government or the relationships to the government. If a definition and evaluation of these factors in modern society affecting academia so markedly can be made, institutions are then faced with the larger questions about the role of the university and the relevance of the university to the world today.

In these terms it was suggested that the Seminar had been discussing the wrong problems, the wrong questions. The basis for this concern was suggested by one participant as follows:

> Whereas we have dealt with the dichotomies and ambiguities of pragmatism and idealism, the reality of the contemporary university is that it finds itself in the process of defining a new conception of a new kind of university. The definition is not yet clear. The answer to the problem of government-academic relationships does not lie in an effort to recover some kind of relationship, which probably never existed, between two ill-defined institutions, but rather in the recognition that both the government and the universities are moving toward a new or changed definition of their purposes more in keeping with the contemporary world and with our ideas of what must be done to meet the problems of the contemporary world. In this context there is a commonality of interests in current problems that is more important than a definition of differences.

The Seminar as a whole did not appear to think that the defining of differences between the government and the university as institutions was a worthwhile enterprise. On the contrary, some stress was placed on the problem-solving approach, on problems common to government and academic institutions, especially in overseas technical assistance activities. The problem-solving approach was discussed in two different ways, first, as providing common interests for cooperative or complementary activities, and second, as providing solutions to common problems which government and institutions share. Seeking solutions to problems in which there is a common interest provides both a reason and a way for government and universities to work together. The interdisciplinary and problem-solving approach has proved very successful in overseas activities, it was noted. For example, if the government comes to the institution with a definite set of problems and asks what resources the institution can bring to bear; then the university can be helpful. Several of the problems in human resource development are precisely the kind where university resources can be useful. Certainly the U.S. institution which has experienced the process of responding to the social, political, economic, and scientific needs for modernization is the ideal mechanism for assisting an institution in a developing country faced with similar kinds of responsibilities.

There are also the common problems which government and institutions share in overseas activities. In a sense each is serving as a model while engaged in overseas technical assistance, and each is therefore faced with the problem of serving as an example of a viable community. Within any such pluralistic community there are factions working at cross purposes vastly complicating the model. The engineer is building dams while the anthropologist is attempting to preserve the culture that will be destroyed in the process, for example. There are problems in gaining an over-all ecological approach to development in any country, and these are shared problems of government and academic institutions. Both are affected. It is important to recognize that there should be a continuum in overseas activities.

It was suggested finally that if there is any crisis in identity, it has not emerged from the university's distorting its mission by undertaking international programs that could better be done by the government, but rather from the failure of the university to find a new relationship to a new kind of world and to develop programs with a new kind of relevance now being demanded of the university in all areas. Learning must in some sense relate to the humanizing of the whole. There is no context in which a university can function other than the international context. No higher purposes can likely be served than realizing the promise of this opportunity and responsibility whether the discussion is concerned with government-academic relations, the realignment of the disciplines, or any other of the major problems of the contemporary university.

The Development of
Coordinated Planning for
International Educational Endeavors

Days of promise and hope may also reflect moods of uncertainty and impatience. There is an anxiety about how well the university will stand up to public international service and about how much inventiveness and endurance will flow from the government. Our conversation is broken occasionally by fitful bursts of dismay. From one side come the rumors of retrenchment in the private sector. On the other falls a gulf between public intention and feasibility. We are worried over what has happened to the sinews which integrate university life, and also about finding those who can bring these sinews back to life. And we are puzzled by the absence of those who would support the university for what it alone may do rather than for what services it may render to satisfy special needs.

Paul A. Miller

We have addressed again an old point of an old debate, the confusions surrounding the university as it carries on its necessary work in the larger community. Public international service joins a great many other hopes now expressed on behalf of the university. We want our interest in international topics to perfuse the general aim of higher education, yet it inevitably presses another claim against the old ethic that a university serves best by somehow remaining free of the momentary requests of society.

Our conversations would direct the university to take itself better in hand, especially in relation to those official bodies in need of services. However, we insist equally that ties between universities and government be sustained. Our discussions show also that we are unclear about how best to balance our trust in the effectiveness of the individual scholar with a trust in the institution where he performs his work. There are three preliminary comments I should like to make about these points so difficult to reconcile especially since they are implicated in the preparations now under way to advance our interests in international education and research.

First, it is obvious that there is no single architect of the categorical support which describes so much of the relationship

115

between the modern university and government. People in general score their requests in specific terms. Educators themselves will protect the subjects of their loyalty by definitions of the most narrow wording. They will organize themselves in a moment in order to defend some special meaning. The greatest suspicion for the community of scholars is not infrequently held by the scholar himself. The political process responds more quickly to the specific claim than to a general one. The game of administrative bifurcation is made possible by a quite human attachment to specifics. In short, all of us contribute to splintering general interests into specific ones.

Second, we have already gone far to shape the American university along categorical lines. My inclination is that inner logic of the university has moved so far from a condition of equilibrium that recapturing something called institutional commitment may now be beyond the genius of most academic men. All of us have become doers, instrumentalists if you will. Those who would foster contact and communication within the academic community have been lost. With instrumentalists at the head of the column, and few integrative people even in the ranks, it is difficult sometimes to see the university for the encrustation of special activity that has been fastened upon it. Sponsorship is now elusive; teaching is tied to local interests, research to national support, and public service to both. It is within such a milieu that we would propose to provoke a commitment to international research and education.

Third, we should remind ourselves of relationships less well developed than the government-academic one. Colleges and universities remain for the most part unconcerned with the lower schools. The American scheme of institutional governance and competition inhibits the good sense of cooperative work among several institutions. While scholars may find their way into a more worldly intellectual community, few ways have been found to help their institutions profit by it. And we encourage all others to think of education in systemic terms, but are prone not to practice it for ourselves.

Just as you would accent the relational problems of universities in devising a future in public international service, so has this issue grown in importance during the planning for the administration of the International Education Act. It is good fortune, indeed, that the law and the supporting legislative language bring the question of relationship squarely to the fore.

Regardless of how it comes by it, the Center for Educational Cooperation must carry on its work of supporting institutions by some form of national plan for international research and education. I do not mean a rigid and inflexible plan, but rather some general principles to guide the national effort forward with reasonable direction. Such an outline should include at least an elementary intelligence about the ends which count, some measure at given moments of capability, and steps which offer promise of multiplying the initial effort. Such a national plan or outline of purpose should be useful to colleges and universities as they cast their own future in international education. It would also seem to be necessary for urging the agencies of the government to work together on common cause.

It is clear to me that both the academic community and the governmental centers involved must join in devising this plan and in keeping it current. While we may expect the National Advisory Committee on International Studies to oversee this activity, having a consensus arise over and over again from the educators will require ways of talking to each other not now apparent in the government-university relationship. How does one lift the academic enterprise and the entire country up to new levels of international competence? This is a question on which some consensus among the institutions of higher learning must be found. The government centers must bring to it a concern for the extent of national and international needs. Both processes should join and both should be continuous. It is to be hoped that neither of them will become final, rather, remaining imprecise as to specification. Devising a national plan challenges the government to respond to new and more general signs of cooperative strength in the academic community.

Planning will depend to great extent upon a sense of overall objective. Whatever the possibilities of the International Education Act, and all of the related programs and resources, they will not be unlocked unless some hierarchy of ends is developed and shared.

The language of the Act clearly sets forth the more immediate and perhaps the most important objective—enlarging the international dimension in the work of students and faculty. It is an aim which must be weighed in terms of the entire system of higher education, while the means to accomplish it must belong to given colleges and universities, independently or in groups. This objective will call for reviews of current practice and experiments with new practices. Such an objective would state that the education of all the people must be preceded by the education of those who would profess to teach them.

The second objective is to cultivate higher education as a national resource of competence about international topics. This aim

117

calls for institutional commitment, an overall design for competence within institutions and in the country as a whole, general and dependable support by government centers, facility for cooperative activity among institutions, and effective assessments of progress.

The third objective would insist that such competence flow steadily into the common culture. By means of more and better curriculum development, together with new visions of teacher education, building up higher education should also enrich the lower schools. No less should be expected of adult education.

The fourth objective, and the ultimate promise of the International Education Act, concerns how best to share the improving competence of the United States within the larger community of educational cooperation. One would expect this sharing to touch with significance the future of technical assistance, the development of institutions, and the elaboration of voluntary projects. It is to be hoped that governments will nurture this activity of wider scale without insisting that it be monitored for purposes other than recognizing the common hopes of people everywhere for the education of their young. It must be pointed out also that improving the competence of any country, insofar as scholarly observations will be made abroad, will likely depend more and more upon the collaboration of scholars. Time would seem to be running out on the short-term exploitation of research opportunities.

So much for a national plan and the hierarchy of ends upon which it might be based! I turn now to some points of procedure, particularly as they refer to cooperation between educators and government representatives.

If institutions as wholes are to become the units of planning, it seems crucially important that appropriate responsibilities be worked out mutually between the educational community and the government centers concerned. Institutions should be asked to plan their own commitments in international education, commitments which are evident to faculty, officers, and trustees alike. Clearly, these institutions selected for support as centers of graduate and research excellence should also perform certain extramural duties—serving as centers of strength for schools and colleges in the immediate region, for trainee programs, for adult education, and public international service while they are progressing as competent centers.

As for government support, it would be my hope that some principle of procedure would assure wide latitudes of choice within institutions, yet explicit constraints defined in terms of institutional plans and the rationale of needs in the country as a whole.

Second, whatever national plan is devised should remain an

open document for debate and further development by all concerned. The National Advisory Committee will want to sponsor this larger discussion, but thought must also be given to ways of stimulating, reviewing, and selecting proposals for assistance. We should also expect the Center for Educational Cooperation to sponsor substantive discussions among scholars to contribute continuously to national planning.

Third, we should set up a five-year period of experimentation and innovation for the undergraduate emphasis of this new effort. Many questions, as yet unanswered, make this part of the task more complex in my view than others. Will the international dimension require a curriculum core? How does one weave area interests and disciplinary views together and then relate them both to problems? How does one establish working groups of faculty who represent several disciplines and then provide travel and training opportunities for them? In the end will the consortium turn out to be useful? How will graduate strength touch undergraduate needs in the more complex institutions? How may one temper unwise haste for curriculum change?

A fourth point of procedure would urge careful coordination of aims and relationships among the various agencies of the government. This is more than a pious hope. I doubt that resources will become so plentiful to make us indifferent to this need. Several streams of support, even with widely varied missions, should be converged through meticulous planning at the point of given institutions.

My fifth point of procedure asks that the outcome of our own growing competence be that of joining with colleagues elsewhere to find fresh ways of advancing a worldwide intellectual community. If this be the ultimate aim of international education, then we in this country should take stock of the limitations of informal communications and more formal cooperation. The implications of this activity are unique to no country, yet common to all of them. Rendering public international service from the vantage point of the academy will find its most natural expression when colleagues elsewhere, individually and by institutions, join in common cause. To circumvent scholarly communication and joint work, without building it up in the bargain, will always be alien to academic people, regardless of the merits of the services requested.

Finally, permit me to reveal in the most candid way a very few troublesome doubts I have about the problems which confront us in international education.

Is it really too much to expect the academic community to speak with consensus about overall planning in a field so diverse as international education? It is unlikely that general institutional

119

support, in even a broadly defined field of international education, will come off, short of formula aid to every college and university, without some way of honoring institutional distinctiveness within some scheme of purpose for the system of higher education as a whole. Already the storm clouds gather, small places fearful of being jostled aside by the large places, weak institutions looking for what they believe to be inequitable allocation, and strong institutions prepared to expose unwise dilution. While conviction and courage will be required of the government, these issues are even more the burden of the academic community. If we could find some way to overcome these problems which get in the way of trust and consensus, a way which would preserve the vigor and uniqueness of independent approaches, a new level of conversation would have been born among academic institutions and federal agencies. Perhaps the continued planning under the International Education Act may make a contribution beyond its own purpose.

Another problem is how best to develop the Center for Educational Cooperation with sufficient yeastiness so that it will merit the interest and confidence of the academic community. Under the best of circumstances, it runs the risk of becoming another government office which has done little more than add its grants to the shopping list. From my view, it should be a competent, reflective, analytical, and courageous place. It should be intimately familiar with academic life in this country, and holding to no boundaries in reaching out to sister agencies, professional societies, and centers of similar design in the international community. Members of the academic community must participate in the creating of such a center.

I am equally if not more anxious over the need for intelligent investment on the one hand, and, on the other, the need to increase the community of interest sufficient for public and political viability. We are talking about elevating the strength of our educational community for the long pull ahead, rather than strengthening research and education as a shorter-term response to the multiplying missions of both the public and private sectors. I hope that we really mean it when we speak of enriching the scholarly community of this country, and thereby playing our part in the enrichment of the educational community throughout the world more fully.

Though there are safeguards in the language of the Act, we shall have also to remain watchful that the efforts supported will remain open and unclassified, committed to both scholarly review and public surveillance. I hope that the Center for Educational Cooperation will always reflect these sentiments now in the official record suggesting that the aims of the Act could not be reconciled with the work of educators not fully a part of the scholarly and public domain.

Finally, I hope this effort will not simply set off a new wave of fads. While invention and innovation are necessary in every aspect of international research and education, it is a field which deserves more than scores of institutional representatives selling one item of novelty or another. To envisage an international point of a view capable of penetrating every corner of a college or university will require innovation and more innovation. But I hope we don't succumb to jabbing about the academic front willy-nilly. Indeed, if the long pull is important, support to the more ponderous and orthodox approaches may, a decade hence, pull ahead of the more exuberant bursts of novelty.

To summarize the ideas I have been discussing, I would set forth these rubrics:

1. If a mutual and natural interaction is to occur among educators and their institutions in the world community, it must be practiced and advanced at home.

2. Cooperation between public and private activity and between academic and nonacademic interests, as well as between government and nongovernment, would seem to be a necessary condition of public international service.

3. International education cannot be evaluated except by standards which are long-term in character. This calls for the element of faith, and we, who have gained so much from the fruits of education, should bear witness to that faith.

4. Whatever the duties which higher education takes on as public international service, whether to share technical knowledge and skill or to function in the more erudite corners of learning, those duties performed with the highest fidelity will leave in their wake a new appreciation of the educator and a stronger basis for scholarship. Only with this condition may colleges and universities do what they alone are best able to do.

We are living at a time when we are called upon to attend to an idea characterized less by its newness than by the need for it. In a time made paradoxical by the presence of unbridled strength and growing gentleness, each of us must find the motive to keep on working with the idea, although its dimness may find us occasionally lost from it. But may we never be lost from the insight that no single bond surpasses education in uniting one man to another, nothing like learning melts the boundaries between generations and nations. Educators are content to live by the language of evidence. It is a language without locus, which makes activity common and international even when it is most dispersed. It is a language which engages an identical faith.

121

Program

American Council on Education Seminar
in Collaboration with the Department of State
International Conference Room, Department of State
March 24, 1967

*Theme: Higher Education and the Public International Service:
The Next Decades–Potentialities and Problems*

Opening Session: The Government–Academic Collaboration
Presiding: Stephen K. Bailey
Introduction: Logan Wilson
Greetings: Secretary of State Dean Rusk

Address: Assistant Secretary of State for
Educational and Cultural Affairs Charles Frankel

Morning Discussion: The de Kiewiet and Harbison Papers
"Government, the Universities, and International Affairs:
The Common Responsibilities" by C. W. de Kiewiet
"The Development and Utilization of Human Resources: Building
a System for Assistance Activities" by Frederick Harbison
Moderator: Stephen K. Bailey
Reviewers: Paul R. Hanna on the de Kiewiet Paper
Royden C. Dangerfield on the Harbison Paper

Afternoon Discussion: The Adams–Jaffe Paper
"Government, the Universities, and International Affairs:
A Crisis in Identity" by Walter Adams and Adrian Jaffe
Moderator: Stephen K. Bailey
Reviewer: Jacob Canter
Rapporteur: Harrison Sasscer

Dinner
Presiding: Logan Wilson
Address: Assistant Secretary for Education Paul A. Miller

122

Participants

WILLIAM C. ACKERMAN
Special Assistant
Office of the Assistant Secretary for
  Educational and Cultural Affairs
Department of State

* WALTER ADAMS
Department of Economics
Michigan State University

GILBERT ANDERSON
Chief, Division for University
  Activities
Office of U.S. Programs and Services
Department of State

GEORGE W. ANGELL
President
State University of New York
  at Plattsburgh

GEORGE E. ARNSTEIN
Project Director
Manpower and Talent Clearing House
  and NEA Search
Washington, D.C.

* STEPHEN K. BAILEY
Dean, School of Citizenship and
  Public Affairs
Syracuse University

CURTIS BARKER
University Relations Office
Agency for International Development

* VINCENT BARNETT
President
Colgate University

DOUGLAS N. BATSON
Deputy Assistant Secretary
Bureau of Educational and Cultural
  Affairs
Department of State

THOMAS P. BERGIN
Dean, Center for Continuing
  Education
University of Notre Dame

CHARLES BLITZER
Director, Division of Education
  and Training
Smithsonian Institution

PAUL J. BRAISTED
President
The Edward W. Hazen Foundation
New Haven, Connecticut

FURMAN BRIDGERS
President
National Association for Foreign
  Student Affairs
University of Maryland

NATHAN BRODSKY
Director for Educational Programs
  and Management Training
Office of Deputy Assistant Secretary
  of Defense for Education
The Pentagon

* JOHN T. CALDWELL
Chancellor, North Carolina State
  University at Raleigh

GWENDOLEN CARTER
Director, Program of African Studies
Northwestern University

* JACOB CANTER
Deputy Assistant Secretary
Bureau of Educational and Cultural
  Affairs
Department of State

WILLIAM G. CARR
Executive Secretary
National Education Association

* R. TAYLOR COLE
Provost
Duke University

* FRANCIS J. COLLIGAN
Director, Policy Review and Research
  Staff
Bureau of Educational and Cultural
  Affairs
Department of State

* Panelist

123

EDUCATION AND PUBLIC INTERNATIONAL SERVICE

EVAN R. COLLINS
President
State University of New York
at Albany

Joseph Colmen
Deputy Assistant Secretary
for Education
Department of Health, Education,
and Welfare

PAUL A. COOK
Senior Foreign Affairs Analysis Officer
Policy Review and Coordination Staff
Bureau of Educational and Cultural
Affairs
Department of State

* WILLIAM CRAIG
Deputy Assistant Secretary for
Health, Education, and Welfare
Department of Health, Education,
and Welfare

MARTIN G. CRAMER
Educational Plans Adviser
Office of Public Services
Department of State

ROYDEN C. DANGERFIELD
Director of International Programs
University of Illinois

* JAMES M. DAVIS
Vice President
Foreign Student Programs
Institute of International Education

WILSON P. DIZARD
Assistant Deputy Director
Office of Policy and Research
U.S. Information Agency

JAMES A. DONOVAN, JR.
Director, Secretariat to the
United States Advisory Commis-
sion on International Educational
and Cultural Affairs
Department of State

ALAN S. DOWNER
Chairman, Department of English
Princeton University

J. H. ESTERLINE
Office of Far Eastern Programs
Bureau of Educational and Cultural
Affairs
Department of State

MICHAEL J. FLACK
Graduate School of Public and
International Affairs
University of Pittsburgh

HARRY FOREMAN
Associate Dean
International Programs
University of Minnesota

* CHARLES FRANKEL
Assistant Secretary of State for
Educational and Cultural Affairs
Department of State

JOHN GANGE
Director
Institute of International Studies
and Overseas Administration
University of Oregon

PETER GILLINGHAM
Executive Associate
Education and World Affairs

MEREDITH GIVENS
Chief, Manpower Planning Branch
Office of Technical Cooperation
and Research
Agency for International Development

SHELTON GRANGER
Deputy Assistant Secretary for
International Affairs
Office of Assistant Secretary for
Education
Department of Health, Education,
and Welfare

* ROBERT G. GREENWAY
Deputy Director
Division of Institutional Relations
Peace Corps

MASON GROSS
President
Rutgers, The State University
New Brunswick, New Jersey

* Panelist

124

JOSEPH HAJDA
Director, International Activities
Kansas State University

SAMUEL HALPERIN
Deputy Assistant Secretary for
    Legislation
Department of Health, Education,
    and Welfare

D. LEE HAMILTON
Acting Director
Division of Foreign Studies
U.S. Office of Education
Department of Health, Education,
    and Welfare

* PAUL R. HANNA
Director, International Development
    Education Center
Stanford University

CARYL P. HASKINS
President
Carnegie Institution of Washington

* H. FIELD HAVILAND
Director of Foreign Policy Studies
The Brookings Institution

RICHARD H. HEINDEL
Dean of Faculty
Capitol Campus
Pennsylvania State University

DAVID D. HENRY
Director
International Office
Harvard University

HENRY BERTRAM HILL
Dean, International Studies and
    Programs
University of Wisconsin

FRANK S. HOPKINS
Director
Office of U.S. Programs and Service
Bureau of Educational and Cultural
    Affairs
Department of State

LOUIS B. HOWARD
Director
International Programs Office
National Association of State
    Universities & Land Grant Colleges

CHARLOTTE MOTON HUBBARD
Deputy Assistant Secretary for
    Public Affairs
Department of State

DAYTON W. HULL
Public Information and Reports Staff
Bureau of Educational and Cultural
    Affairs
Department of State

EDMOND C. HUTCHINSON
Research Council
Research Analysis Corporation
McLean, Virginia

J. ROLAND JACOBS
Director, Office of African Programs
Bureau of Educational and Cultural
    Affairs
Department of State

* ADRIAN JAFFE
Professor of English and Comparative
    Literature
Michigan State University

HUGH M. JENKINS
Executive Director
National Association for Foreign
    Student Affairs

* ELDON L. JOHNSON
Vice President
University of Illinois

WILLIAM B. JONES
Director, Office of Program Evaluation
    and Analysis Staff
Bureau of Educational and Cultural
    Affairs
Department of State

WILLIAM C. KELLY
Director
Fellowship Office
National Academy of Sciences

* Panelist

125

A. KHOSHKISH
Associate Professor of
    Political Science
Moorhead State College

CHARLES V. KIDD
Office of Science and Technology
Executive Office of the President
Washington, D.C.

ROBERT C. LEESTMA
Director, Office of Multilateral
    Policy and Programs
Bureau of Educational and Cultural
    Affairs
Department of State

KATIE LOUCHHEIM
Deputy Assistant Secretary of State for
    Educational and Cultural Affairs
Department of State

STEEN MCCALL
Deputy Director
Education and Manpower Planning
    Service
Agency for International Development

GERARD J. MANGONE
Director, International Organization
    Research Program
Maxwell Graduate School of Citizen-
    ship and Public Affairs
Syracuse University

HAROLD MILLER
Policy Review and Coordination Staff
Bureau of Educational and Cultural
    Affairs
Department of State

* PAUL A. MILLER
Assistant Secretary for Education
Department of Health, Education,
    and Welfare

ALBERT H. MOSEMAN
Assistant Administrator for Technical
    Cooperation and Research
Agency for International Development

J. RALPH MURRAY
President
Elmira College

JULIAN L. NUGENT
Director
Office of Inter-American Programs
Bureau of Educational and Cultural
    Affairs
Department of State

JAMES NUSSMAN
Secretary
Overseas Liaison Committee
American Council on Education

GLENN A. OLDS
Executive Dean
International Studies & World Affairs
State University of New York
    at Planting Fields

VICTOR RAPPORT
Dean for International Studies
Wayne State University

ELINOR P. REAMS
Assistant Director
Policy Review and Coordination Staff
Bureau of Educational and Cultural
    Affairs
Department of State

ANDRE E. RHEAULT
Washington Representative
Education and World Affairs

* ALVIN ROSEMAN
Associate Dean
Graduate School of Public and
    International Affairs
University of Pittsburgh

ROBERT M. ROSENZWEIG
Director, Center for Research
    in International Studies
Stanford University

RALPH W. RUFFNER
Vice President
Southern Illinois University

ROBERT RUPARD
Director, Office of Institutional
    Development
Bureau for Africa
Agency for International Development

* Panelist

126

PARTICIPANTS

DEAN RUSK
Secretary, U.S. Department of State

EDWARD SANDERS
Vice President & Director of the
Washington Office
College Entrance Examination Board

HARRISON SASSCER
Program Director
Association of American Colleges

KENNEDY B. SCHMERTZ
Director, Foreign Currency Program
Office of International Activities
Smithsonian Institution

FREDERICK SEITZ
President
National Academy of Sciences

GEORGE SELTZER
Industrial Relations Center
University of Minnesota

E. JOSEPH SHOBEN, JR.
Director, Commission on Academic
Affairs
American Council on Education

ALBERT G. SIMS
Vice President
College Entrance Examination Board

JOHN J. SLOCUM
Cultural Affairs Adviser
Office of Policy and Research
United States Information Agency

PAUL E. SMITH
Secretary, Committee on International
Relations
National Education Association

SETH SPAULDING
International Education Programs
University of Pittsburgh

STEPHEN H. STACKPOLE
Executive Associate
Carnegie Corporation of New York

BASCOM STORY
Director, Education and Manpower
Planning Service
Agency for International Development

WILLIAM H. TAFT III
International Scientific and
Technological Affairs
Department of State

M. H. TRYTTEN
Director, Office of Scientific
Personnel
National Academy of Sciences

* JOHN USEEM
Department of Sociology and
Anthropology
Michigan State University

RUTH USEEM
Department of Sociology
Michigan State University

ROBERT VAN DUYN
Office of Institutional Development
Africa-Europe Bureau
Agency for International Development

MYRON VENT
Chief, Educational Planning Branch
Office of Technical Cooperation
and Research
Agency for International Development

RALPH VOGEL
Director, Operations Staff
Bureau of Educational and Cultural
Affairs
Board of Foreign Scholarships
Department of State

GEORGE WAGGONER
Dean, College of Arts and Sciences
University of Kansas

WILLIAM W. WARNER
Director, Office of International
Activities
Smithsonian Institution

* Panelist

127

RANDALL M. WHALEY
Chancellor, University of Missouri
at Kansas City

FRANCIS WILCOX
Dean, School of Advanced
International Studies
Johns Hopkins University

LOGAN WILSON
President
American Council on Education

C. TYLER WOOD
Special Assistant
Office of the Administrator
Agency for International Development

* F. L. WORMALD
Vice President
Association of American Colleges

GERALD YATES, S. J.
Director, International Student
Programs
Georgetown University

FRANCIS A. YOUNG
Executive Secretary
Committee on International Exchange
of Persons

Conference Board of Associated
Research Councils
Washington, D.C.

STAFF

RICHARD A. HUMPHREY
Director, Commission on International
Education
American Council on Education

ELIZABETH SHIVER
Staff Assistant
Commission on International
Education
American Council on Education

LESLIE SIEBERT
Secretary to the Director
Commission on International Education
American Council on Education

* Panelist

128

American Council on Education
Logan Wilson, President

The American Council on Education, founded in 1918, is a
council of educational organizations and institutions. Its purpose
is to advance education and educational methods through comprehensive voluntary and cooperative action on the part of American
educational associations, organizations, and institutions.